The handbook of clinical supervision: your questions answered

The handbook of clinical supervision: your questions answered

Edited by
John Fowler

Quay
Books

610.730⁷ Fow

UCSM

Quay Books, Division of Mark Allen Publishing Limited Jesses Farm, Snow Hill, Dinton, Nr Salisbury, Wilts, SP3 5HN

Mark Allen Publishing Ltd. 1998

ISBN 1–85642–055 8

British Cataloguing-in-Publication Data A catalogue record for this book is available from the Bristish Library

Printed in the UK by RedwoodBooks, Trowbridge, Wiltshire.

Contents

Contributors   ix

Acknowledgements   xiii

Foreword   xv

Preface   xvii

How to use this book   xix

Chapter 1 - Demystifying clinical supervision

What is clinical supervision?   1

What is the difference between mentoring,
preceptorship and clinical supervision?   5

What does the UKCC say about clinical supervision?   10

What does the Department of Health say about
clinical supervision?   13

Is clinical supervision about inspection and control?   16

Is clinical supervision only about clinical practice?   18

Is clinical supervision new?   22

Our area has some form of clinical supervision,
does it have to change?   24

Do we really need clinical supervision?   26

Is clinical supervision compulsory for all staff?   28

Is clinical supervision the same as the
supervision that students receive?   30

What is the difference between clinical supervision
and individual performance review?   34

Is there a connection between clinical supervision
and counselling? 36

Is there a connection between clinical supervision
and reflective practice? 39

Should health care assistants receive clinical
supervision? 42

What is the cost of clinical supervision? 43

Chapter 2 - Implementing clinical supervision

How do you develop a system of clinical supervision
to meet your needs? 47

How does the ward manager go about implementing
clinical supervision? 51

How does a health care manager implement clinical
supervision? 55

Do different groups of people need to use different
models of clinical supervision? 59

Are there different models of clinical supervision? 62

Process models of clinical supervision 65

Should there be a hospital or Trust model of clinical
supervision? 67

What is the role of the clinical supervisor? 70

What is your role as a supervisee? 74

Can you choose who will be your supervisor? 76

Can the line manager be the supervisor? 77

Is there an optimum number of people that one
person can supervise? 80

What sort of training should supervisors have? 82

Chapter 3 - Individual sessions of clinical supervision

What do you do after you say hello? 85

Should clinical supervision sessions have an agenda? 90

Is clinical supervision confidential? 94

Should records of clinical supervision be kept? 96

How much time should be allocated for clinical supervision? 98

What does it feel like to be supervised? 101

What does it feel like to be a clinical supervisor? 103

Suppose you do not get on with your supervisor/supervisee? 105

Chapter 4 - Working examples

How could it work for a staff nurse working in mental health? 108

How could it work for a ward manager on a general medical ward? 110

How could it work for a district nurse? 113

How could it work for a staff nurse in a learning disability group home? 119

How could it work for health care assistants? 121

How could it work for a clinical nurse specialist? 123

How could it work for a sister charge nurse on a children's ward? 126

How could it work for a staff nurse on an intensive care unit? 128

How could it work for a health visitor? 131

How could it work for a practice nurse 137

How could it work for a someone working in a nursing home? 142

Chapter 5 - Evaluating the benefits of clinical supervision

How does clinical supervision benefit the supervisee?   147

How does clinical supervision benefit the supervisor?   150

How does clinical supervision benefit the clinical area?   151

How does clinical supervision benefit the hospital/ Trust?   154

How does clinical supervision benefit patients/ clients?   157

Appendix I

A contract for clinical supervision   160

Appendix II

Evaluating a clinical supervision session   164

References   168

Index   175

Contributors

Andrew Clark - RMN RGN CPN Cert FETC ENB 955 DMS MBA

Andrew commenced his RMN training in 1976 in the North East of England and after completing his general nurse training in 1983 returned to psychiatry. He has held various posts and worked in a number of districts and has an interest in clinical supervision dating back to the mid eighties when he was a Community Psychiatric Nurse. His other posts have included Clinical Nurse Manager (Community) and in addition has spent five years managing in patient services as a Clinical Nurse Manager and Patient Services Manager. He is currently working as a Practice Development Nurse (Community) in Leicestershire. His interests outside work include music and nature.

Jim Dooher - RMN FHE Cert. Ed Dip HCR. MA. Senior Lecturer School of Health and Community Studies. Subject Leader for Mental Health Diploma. Honorary Practice Development Nurse, Leicestershire Mental Health Service NHS Trust.

Having commenced his nurse training in 1980 Jim worked in a variety of psychiatric settings and went on to specialise in rehabilitation nursing, leading a team dedicated to providing the skills necessary for successful discharge into the community. He went on to take up the role of Practice Development Nurse where he developed a multidisciplinary course for clinical supervision, which over the past four years has evolved to meet the needs of the local Trust. Jim is heavily involved in the evaluation of clinical supervision through a collaborative research project.

Chris Hale - RGN PN Cert. Moorfields Cert. ITEC Nurse Advisor, Primary Care, Leicestershire Health.

On qualifying in Hertfordshire Chris practised in general surgery, gynaecology and operating theatre, specialising in ophthalmology. After a period of travelling abroad she moved to primary care gaining a variety of practice nursing experience in both rural and inner city environments. The frequently part time nature of this role also enabled her to work in areas as diverse as teaching neonatal resuscitation and practising as a complementary therapist. In 1993 she moved to Leicestershire as Practice Nurse Facilitator where she was involved in developing the BSc Hons. Community Health Nursing with De Montfort University by both writing the General Practice Nursing module and devising a new system of practice teachers for General Practice.

   She is presently developing clinical supervision for Leicestershire practice nurses incorporating both training and reimbursement for clinical supervisors.

Kim Jacobs - RGN RHV MA. Director of Nursing, Independent Sector.

Since qualifying, Kim has held a variety of posts, including health visiting, practice nursing and community management. In 1992 Kim moved into the independent sector currently working as a Director of Nursing. She is undertaking an MSc in Advanced

Nursing Practice and has a special interest in clinical supervision.

Ann-Marie Phillips - RGN Dip N. BA (Hons) MA. Professional Development Nurse, Medical directorate, Leicester General Hospital NHS Trust.

Ann-Marie qualified in 1989 and has worked on a variety of medical wards. Ann-Marie was the site coordinator in the National Clinical Supervision Evaluation Project led by Manchester University. She was also the ward manager of the study site responsible for implementing clinical supervision and has first hand experience of the effects of introducing clinical supervision into a busy ward.

Ann-Marie has a keen interest in nursing education and research. She is a module leader on the BSc in Community Nursing at De Montfort University and is currently registered for a PhD.

Ann-Marie has one son and enjoys a variety of sports.

Rachel North - RGN RHV DPSN BA (Hons) Senior Nurse Professional Development, Fosse Health NHS Trust, Leicester.

Rachel qualified in 1981 and worked for 5 years in the acute sector, principally in oncology. She then moved into health visiting, practising as a family health visitor before taking up a post as a research health visitor carrying out research related to Sudden Infant Death Syndrome. She now works as a senior nurse in a large community Trust. An important part of her role in professional development has been working with others to implement clinical supervision for all clinical practitioners in the Trust.

Sue Staples - RGN. Senior Nurse, Education and Training, Glenfield Hospital NHS Trust, Leicester.

Since qualifying in 1971 Sue has practised in two Leicester Hospitals, specialising in operating theatre practice. In 1986 she moved to Glenfield Hospital as a theatre sister and later into the posts of clinical manager and then practice development nurse. Her keen interest in education led to her current appointment in the Trusts Department of Nursing and PAMS, responsible for planning and purchasing post registration education.

Sue has a particular interest in clinical supervision and is involved in a project to implement and evaluate clinical supervision within the Trust. Sue is married with two grown up children and enjoys walking and cycling.

Alison Wells - RGN RM Dip.N. Dip. Ed. BA (Hons). Training and Development Manager, Medical Directorate, Leicester Royal Infirmary, NHS Trust.

Alison qualified in 1983 and specialised in medical nursing. In 1987 she qualified as a midwife but returned to general nursing as a ward manager in the medical directorate. Since 1995 Alison has worked as a training and development manager and is responsible for all groups of staff within the medical directorate.

Alison developed an interest in clinical supervision after writing a dissertation on the subject as part of the Postgraduate Diploma in Education. She has also been involved in setting up clinical supervision within the Leicester Royal Infirmary, NHS Trust.

Acknowledgements

To our families, friends and colleagues and all the staff in Leicester whose questions have inspired this book.

Foreword

A few nurses and managers are already acting as powerful ambassadors for clinical supervision. Others although keen to implement it do not know how to do so. Some are unsure about the value of it, others believe that they have *'always done it'*. A small number of very honest practitioners openly acknowledge that they find the whole idea much to threatening to embrace.

We should not be surprised by this uneven response because individuals respond to change in many different ways. Lack of knowledge and fear represent major barriers to personal change. Although clinical supervision is still in its infancy within our profession it is plagued by confusion. Nursing is an extremely diverse profession and new arrangements must be introduced in ways that are appropriate to the specific environment of care.

We clearly need to develop a shared understanding about the principles that underpin clinical supervision and accept that these can be achieved in many different ways. This remarkably helpful handbook draws together frequently asked questions and provides coherent answers. The nine members of the focus group who contributed to this book represent a wide variety of nursing practice. By describing their experiences of clinical supervision and providing practical examples of *'how to do it'* they illustrate both the opportunities and constraints, and by doing so they reduce some of the mystiques associated with it.

Nursing is a complex, challenging and rewarding profession. Practitioners experience pressure from a range of sources, including for example, a difficult workload, the need to learn new skills, rapid turnover of patients, unrealistic expectations, tensions between theory and practice and team dynamics. We all recognise the emotional cost of caring — clinical supervision has the potential to help us to deal with this constructively by enabling the growth of both competence and confidence. Practitioners — and ultimately their patients — will benefit from this process.

Clinical supervision is something that we should all have access to and be prepared to offer. Its introduction should be greeted with enthusiasm by managers and clinicians. This handbook debunks the rhetoric relating to it and explains how to make it work in the real — often imperfect — world.

Cathy McCargow

Chief Nursing Advisor

Leicestershire Health Authority

Preface

The idea of clinical supervision is very simple. It is a relationship which combines support, guidance and feedback for the benefit of the practitioner, their clinical practice and ultimately patient or client care.

Some people will say, *'this is nothing new, we have always done this'*. However when was the last time you seriously discussed issues involved in your current practice or when was the last time someone was genuinely interested in how you coped during a difficult clinical situation? We might know what to do, but how often do we do it?

As well as having very direct benefits for the health care workforce and subsequent patient and client care, clinical supervision has the potential to be one of the most powerful influences on the development of the under-pinning knowledge of the profession.

We often talk about applying theory to practice and evidence based practice, implying that the 'right' answers are in a journal or book, and we need to review the evidence and if appropriate apply the theory to practice. While this is true for much of our work, particularly the objectively measurable parts such as infection control or wound healing, how true is it for all of our work.

'The truth is out there' is a key phrase of science fiction writing, implying that we need to open our minds and look at things from a different perspective. If clinical supervision was established as a dominant culture within health care, then not only could we use it to examine the application of theory to practice, but also to draw out from practice, theories which are alive and relevant to clinical practice. The truth is out there in clinical practice,

and clinical supervision can help to reveal these important truths.

What is clinical supervision ?

Clinical supervision is a practice-focused relationship involving an individual or a group of practitioners reflecting on practice, guided by a skilled supervisor.

Who is a skilled supervisor ? - It could be you!

A skilled supervisor is a qualified health care practitioner who has undergone some preparation. He/she will have an understanding of his/her role and the practice of clinical supervision together with its application to the working environment.

Who is clinical supervision for? - Its for you!

Every practitioner should have an awareness of what clinical supervision has to offer to his/her own working practice, and access to clinical supervision.

How to use this book

This book is designed to be dipped into at any page you open. We do not advise you to open it at the first page and then read it like a novel. There are over fifty questions each with a self contained answer. The answers vary in length, but you should be able to read each answer in about five minutes.

We suggested you browse through the list of questions, note two or three which are of particular interest and then read these first. If you are already using clinical supervision in your clinical area then you may want to focus on certain sections in greater depth. Likewise if you are only just beginning to 'grapple' with it you may want to focus on different areas.

There are a number of 'Working examples', all beginning, 'How could it work for...' You should be able to identify with one of these examples, but do not ignore the rest. Just because you do not work in a learning disability environment does not mean that the model of clinical supervision described could not be used in your area. It is worth reading through all the working examples to see what ideas you can pick up. The examples are not meant to be blueprints, so feel free to question and develop the ideas within the handbook.

Some of the answers within this book draw heavily from articles, books and other published material. Others draw heavily from experience of the contributor, each of whom is directly involved in the implementation of clinical supervision within their own particular clinical speciality. Most contributors draw from both sources with the nature of the question determining the style of the answer.

We have tried to answer the questions honestly and simply, but not simplistically. This may mean that you have tried to read an answer a few times to understand the arguments being put forward. Other questions are more straightforward and the answers can be grasped immediately. Try using some of the questions to prompt discussion in small working groups. Clinical supervision involves discussion and reflection, so why not use some of the questions and answers to get the team thinking.

1

Demystifying Clinical Supervision

Jim Dooher, John Fowler, Ann-Marie Phillips, Rachel North and Alison Wells

What is clinical supervision?

You will already have some ideas as to what you think clinical supervision is. This may result from either personal experience or from reading the literature. You may have developed a well formed understanding or you may have just a few vague ideas. It may be useful to read the following definitions of clinical supervision and compare with your understanding of the term:

- Clinical supervision brings practitioners and skilled supervisors together to reflect on practice. Supervision aims to identify solutions to problems, improve practice and increase understanding of professional issues (UKCC, 1996)

- Clinical supervision is a formal arrangement that enables nurses, midwives and health visitors to discuss their work regularly with another experienced professionals. Clinical supervision involves reflecting upon practice in order to learn from experience and improve competence. An important part of the supervisors role is to facilitate reflection and the learning process (King's Fund. Nursing development units, Kohner, 1994)

- Clinical supervision - a term used to describe a formal process of professional support and learning which enables individual practitioners to develop knowledge and competence, assume responsibility for their own practice and enhance consumer protection and safety of care in complex clinical situations. It is central to the process of learning and to the scope of professional practice and should be seen as a means of encouraging self assessment and analytical and reflective skills (Department of Health, *A Vision for the Future*, 1993)

- In their book on clinical supervision and mentorship in nursing Butterworth and Faugier (1992) acknowledge that there are dangers in trying to give a tight definition to clinical supervision however as a working definition they define it as, *'an exchange between practising professionals to enable the development of professional skills'*

- Clinical supervision, *'an interpersonal process where a skilled practitioner helps a less skilled or experienced practitioner to achieve professional abilities appropriate to his role. At the same time they are offered counsel and support'* (Barber and Norman, 1987)

- Clinical supervision is a practice - focused relationship involving an individual or a group of practitioners reflecting on practice, guided by a skilled practitioner. (author's definition, based on the UKCC, 1996).

You can see from these definitions that there is no one all encompassing definition of clinical supervision. This is not because no-one has given serious thought to the subject or that some of these definitions are wrong. Rather it is because the idea of clinical supervision has developed over a number of years from various areas of clinical practice. Since about 1992 a number of people and influential bodies have recognised the need to talk and discuss the process that clinical supervision covers more formally. In order to do this they have tried to define what they mean by the term.

Clinical supervision for the junior staff nurse working in a surgical ward will need to be very different from that of an experienced mental health nurse working in the community. If someone tried to develop or impose one model of clinical supervision and suggested that this should be used for all types of health care situations and all staff irrespective of their experience the result would be of little or no use to anyone.

How does all this help us with our understanding of what clinical supervision is? Firstly, it tells us that clinical supervision is not just some new theoretical idea, it has developed over a period of time and has been influenced by people's clinical practice. Secondly, it tells us that there is no one model of clinical supervision that is appropriate for all. Different groups of staff will want to develop clinical supervision to meet their specific needs. Thirdly, we can conclude that the focus of clinical supervision should be determined locally by clinical staff while the process is facilitated through various management and professional structures.

Although there are differences in the previous definitions there are underlying principles that help us identify just what clinical supervision could cover. These are:

- At least two people are involved in meeting together with a specific purpose of discussing clinical practice. The general assumption is that one of these people is more experienced than the other, although there are examples where clinical supervision involves a small group of people or when both practitioners have similar experiences

- Another theme that is common to these definitions is that they not only talk about practice but that they also reflect upon it. Reflection upon practice requires structure, focus and objectivity.

The combination of at least two people meeting together to reflect upon practice requires a degree of organisation or formality that is not a traditional part of nursing culture. We may often meet together to review a patient's care but this is usually at a level of discussion rather than reflection and so tends to focus on immediate problem-solving rather than analysis of previous practice.

Table 1.1: Principles of clinical supervision

At least two people meeting together for the purpose of clinical supervision

Using 'reflection' to focus upon clinical practice

The meetings are structured and organised.

If these are the principles of clinical supervision the next question you are probably asking is what is its purpose? If you review the earlier definitions again you will see that there is not just one purpose to clinical supervision but the possibility of three:

1. It is a learning process
2. It is a supportive process
3. It is a monitoring process.

It may be that clinical supervision as it is developed for one group of practitioners takes on a predominantly supportive process, while for another group the learning process is the most important and for yet for another group it is a combination of all that defines the purpose of clinical supervision for them.

Figure 1.1: Process of clinical supervision

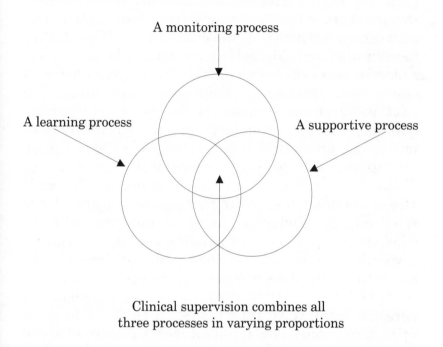

A monitoring process

A learning process

A supportive process

Clinical supervision combines all
three processes in varying proportions

So what is clinical supervision? Clinical supervision is a practice–focused relationship involving an individual or a group of practitioners reflecting on practice, guided by a skilled supervisor. While definitions are useful to aid common understanding, what you need to think through is the important principles and purpose of clinical supervision for you in your clinical area and then define your aim for clinical supervision.

What is the difference between mentoring, preceptorship and clinical supervision?

All of these terms are used quite frequently within our daily practice. Some people will use the terms interchangeably recognising little or no difference between them. This is understandable as they all have a common theme. There is however some fairly distinct differences between them which will be discussed later. What do they have in common? Mentoring, preceptorship and clinical supervision are all about a relationship normally between two people, although it could be a small group. The relationship focuses upon the needs of one person, normally this is about an experienced practitioner mentoring, precepting or supervising a less experienced practitioner, although peer supervision, two practitioners of similar experience, can be a useful practice. There is also a common feature regarding the nature of the relationship, obviously any relationship will be dependant upon the personality of the individuals involved but in general these relationships can be summed up by the principle, *'they have time for me'*. Many of the relationships in our professional or personal life involve compromise in terms of focusing upon each others needs, indeed it is a feature of social maturity that people can put the meeting of their needs to one side whilst they focus upon the needs of another. The final area that mentoring, preceptorship and clinical supervision have in common is that the relationship has a particular purpose. This purpose, whatever it is, is the reason for the mentoring, preceptorship or clinical supervision.

Table 1.2: Areas common to mentoring, preceptorship and clinical supervision

They all involve a relationship between two people or a small group

The relationship focuses on the needs of one of the people

'They have time for me' is a phrase that sums up the nature of the relationship

The relationship is set up for a particular purpose

Mentor

Mentor is a commonly used term in nursing practice although it tends to lack any precise meaning. Butterworth and Faugier (1992) usefully defined it as, *'an experienced professional nurturing and guiding the novitate'*. Despite the term having fairly widespread use within the profession there is considerable confusion regarding what it means in everyday practice and lack of conformity regarding the nature of mentorship (Maggs, 1994). Within the United Kingdom it frequently refers to the relationship a qualified person has with a student on placement. The ENB (1993) regulations for training state that it is,

> *An appropriately qualified and experienced first level nurse/midwife/or health visitor who, by example and facilitation, guides, assists and supports the student in learning new skills, adopting new behaviour and acquiring new attitudes.*

An interesting study on nurses experiences of mentoring students (Atkins and Williams, 1995) indicates that the role is probably more complex than is commonly acknowledged. The authors identify the time and energy

consuming nature of mentoring, the need for commitment and formal preparation, such as the ENB 998 -
Teaching and assessing course. An interesting point that
this study makes is that the benefits to mentors are not
widely recognised. They found that,

> ...*mentoring is potentially an experience which
> enhances the personal and professional learning and
> development of mentors.*

The study suggests that the development the mentor
experiences should be acknowledged in terms of portfolios
and possibly credits through an APEL scheme.

A study which looked at the views of a small group of
students (Earnshaw, 1995) found that mentors served
numerous roles including role model and socialising
agent. Earnshaw's findings also indicate that this role is
probably more involved than is commonly acknowledged.
The relationship between the mentor and mentee is not a
static one, as the mentee becomes more experienced and
near to qualification the relationship becomes one of
partnership and again becomes mutually beneficial.

American nurses tend to see mentoring in a different
way. Puetz (1985) states that mentoring relationships
can begin at any time and usually last many years. She
sees mentoring on a continuum from role modelling
through preceptorship to mentoring. Role modelling,
being a fairly passive way of learning and teaching,
preceptorship becoming more active and taking on a
coaching role. Mentoring is an ongoing relationship
involving trust and intimacy, where the trusted guide
trains a protégé focusing particularly on their career.'
Further analysis from America includes Darling's
(1984) work in which she identifies three main
characteristics of the mentoring role. Firstly, the mentor
is someone who 'inspires' the mentee with a 'vision' of

what to aim for, secondly as an 'investor', someone who believes in the mentee and communicates that belief and finally as a 'supporter', the mentor providing encouragement and reassurance thus developing confidence. Therefore while mentoring within the UK tends to refer to a teaching and supportive relationship between a student and a qualified practitioner, within America mentoring tends to refer to a long term relationship not restricted to students, in which the mentor takes on a protégé in which the aims are directed to more long term career plans.

Preceptorship

This term is a recent introduction into the UK nursing language, via the UKCC PREP proposal (1990).

> *A newly qualified nurse/midwife/health visitor, or a qualified nurse moving to an unfamiliar clinical area, should have, for at least four months, a preceptor who will help him or her to adjust to that new role.* (UKCC,1993)

The UKCC requires that this should have been introduced as a matter of 'good practice'. There appears to be general agreement that preceptorship intially includes orientation to the work environment, and then teaching, particularly with regards to the routine work of the clinical area. The general aim of preceptorship being to reduce what Kramer (1974) called the *'reality shock'*. Whereas the focus of mentoring is an intimate relationship which aims at assisting the protégé in their career development over a number of years , the focus in preceptorship is in teaching and supporting the person during a specific transition period in their career.

Clinical supervision

As discussed under the heading What is clinical supervision?, the principles are that at least two people are involved in meeting together with a specific purpose of discussing clinical practice, and that they not only talk about clinical practice but also reflect upon it. Reflection upon practice requires structure, focus and objectivity. Butterworth and Faugier (1992) raised the profession's awareness of the need for a more formalised system of clinical supervision and helped to develop a broader understanding of the term. Clinical supervision formally became part of nursing language in *The Vision for the Future* (Department of Health, 1992) that included a definition which incorporated development, support and monitoring of standards. This was subsequently expanded in a UKCC position paper on the subject (UKCC, 1996). Clinical supervision within the UK seems to be encouraging a relationship that has the intimacy and commitment identified with the American perception of mentoring, but is directed more specifically at the supervisees current professional practice. Whereas preceptorship is aimed at a specific transitional period, clinical supervision is ongoing. However, a person at the beginning of their career will want different things from clinical supervision compared to someone who has been in practice for fifteen years. That is why it is difficult to define one set of 'outcomes' of clinical supervision which would be relevant to all staff.

What does the UKCC say about clinical supervision?

In April 1996 the UKCC issued a 'Position statement on clinical supervision for nursing and health visiting

(UKCC, 1996). This followed a period of consultation with the profession regarding the nature of clinical supervision and also if the title 'clinical supervision' was indeed the best term.

The councils statement identifies 6 key statements forming the principles which contribute to the development of a system of clinical supervision at local levels. The UKCC state that,

The incorporation of the key statements into systems of clinical supervision will allow more effective professional development of nurses and health visitors. This will assist patients and clients to receive high quality safe care in a rapidly changing service environment.

Whereas supervision is an integral part of midwifery practice and forms part of the statutory function of the supervisor of midwives (UKCC, 1993a; UKCC, 1994), clinical supervision for nurses and health visitors is not to be a statutory requirement, although this position may be reviewed, 'if the need arises'. Although not compulsory the UKCC state that all practitioners should have access to clinical supervision throughout their careers.

No one model of clinical supervision is proposed by the UKCC, they feel that local needs should influence the development of a model to fit that particular purpose. However, the UKCC are quite clear that it is not a managerial control system and say that *it is not:*

- the exercise of overt managerial responsibility or managerial supervision

- a system of formal individual performance review

- hierarchical in nature.

Table 1.3: The UKCC's six key statements

1. Clinical supervision supports practice, enabling practitioners to maintain and promote standards of care

2. Clinical supervision is a practice-focused professional relationship involving a practitioner reflecting on practice guided by a skilled supervisor

3. The process of clinical supervision should be developed by practitioners and managers according to local circumstances. Ground rules should be agreed so that practicioners and supervisors approach clinical supervision openly, confidently and aware of what is involved

4. Every practioner should have access to clinical supervision. Each supervisor should supervise a realistic number of practioners

5. Preparation for supervisors can be effected using in house or external education programmes. The principles and relevance of clinical supervision should be included in pre- and post registration programmes

6. Evaluation of clinical supervision is needed to assess how it influences care, practice standards and the service. Evaluation systems should be determined locally.

The UKCC endorses the development of clinical supervision. They see it as a way of maintaining and improving standards of care and commend it to practitioners, managers and those involved in negotiating contracts within the health and social care environments.

What does the Department of Health say about clinical supervision?

The emotional cost of caring, the Allitt enquiry (1991) and the recognition that nurses need support and development after registration, gave momentum to the Department of Health's promotion of clinical supervision. This process was already an integral part of practice in some health care professions. To gain a better understanding of how clinical supervision may help develop the clinical practice of nurses, a comprehensive literature review was conducted for the Department of Health (Butterworth and Faugier, 1992) which resulted in the position paper that was disseminated to the profession.

National nursing documents such as *The Vision for the Future* (DoH,1993), promoted and encouraged nurses to implement and develop supervision. The document defines clinical supervision as:

> *...a term used to describe a formal process of professional support and learning which enables individual practitioners to develop knowledge and competence, assume responsibility for their own protection and to enhance consumer protection and the safety of care in complex clinical situations.*

(DoH, 1993).

This document recommended that supervision should be developed and become and integral part of the working life of nurses. The Department of Health has not been prescriptive about how supervision should be introduced and recognises that this must be left to the individual practitioners, as it is dependent upon their own and service need. Target 10 in *The Vision of the Future* (DoH, 1993) stressed that:

Discussions should be held at local and national level on the range and appropriateness of models of clinical supervision.

The Chief Nursing Officer reinforced the Department's commitment to clinical supervision in a letter 94(5) stating,

I have no doubt as to the value of clinical supervision and consider it to be fundamental to safeguarding standards, the development of professional expertise and the delivery of care.

The Department of Health adopted three main approaches to enable the profession to learn more about the issues and principles surrounding supervision:

- Literature, study days and lectures have been supported by the Department to disseminate knowledge about clinical supervision

- They have consulted widely and asked the profession to comment about the way forward and the issues surrounding implementation of supervision

- The Department has supported research to try to enhance and increase knowledge about clinical supervision.

Events Commissioned by the Department of Health included:

- May 1994 the Department of Health sent questionnaires to Trust nurse executives regarding a workshop on clinical supervision. In September two workshops were held and the proceedings were analysed and circulated (Butterworth and Bishop, 1994)

- November 1994 the Department of Health funded a national conference in Birmingham, which was very

successful. The proceedings were then published
(DoH, 1995)

- The 'Triple project' named by Professor Veronica
Bishop is funded by the Department of Health. This
consisted of:

  - A seminar on evaluation techniques which was held
  in March 1995.

  - An invitation to all nurse executives to tender for
  one of the clinical supervision evaluation project
  sites. This part of the project commenced in April
  1995 and was to run for 9 months. However this was
  extended so that more data and information could
  be gained from the project.

  - The third part of the project is the aggregation of
  data, analysis and dissemination (Butterworth *et al*
  1997).

Funding from the Department of Health has enabled
Manchester University to research many aspects of
clinical supervision. The data gathered included information about implementing supervision, the
practical problems that practitioners have experienced
and the effect that supervision has had on both
supervisors and supervisees (Butterworth *et al*, 1997).
Manchester University have also produced briefing
papers for nurses which give information and advice
about implementing clinical supervision, clinical
supervision models and the training and education of
supervisors and supervisees.

The Department of Health does recognise the
potential of this process and how nurses could benefit,
but they remain realistic to the problems of implementing
clinical supervision, and have worked closely with the
profession to try and help address some of these
challenging issues.

Is clinical supervision about inspection and control?

The simple answer to this question is no, particularly if you see it as someone else inspecting and controlling your clinical working practice. However, the answer may be yes if you view it as a process which enables you to develop your own self-awareness, self-inspection and self-control.

The organisation you work for has a responsibility to deliver and maintain high quality services, and clinical supervision is considered to be one way of assuring you are supported in achieving this goal.

As a person who has contact with patients and clients you too have an obligation to ensure the interventions you provide conform to good practice guidelines. Good practice guidelines such as the *Code of Professional Conduct* (UKCC, 1992) and *Professional Education* set out the parameters of what is expected of you in both clinical and to some extent personal settings. These may be complemented by local policies, procedures and philosophies, and you job description. These state your employers intentions and their expectations of how you conduct yourself and what you do during the working day. By agreeing to take up employment and signing a contract you have committed yourself to the controls set out in these documents.

These controls and general oversight of your employment are administered through managerial processes and should not play a direct part in the interactions which occur during your clinical supervision. The substance and content of your clinical supervision sessions should not normally be open to external inspection, it is the property of yourself and your supervisor. It may help both you and your supervisor to keep records of your discussions and any outcomes which are achieved. (This will be considered under the heading: 'Should records of clinical supervision be kept?').

External audit is increasingly becoming an integral part of our working lives. Audits generally measure against an agreed standard, some of which may have been already set by your purchasers and management. With regard to clinical supervision, it may be useful to consider some of the gains for both your employer and purchasers of services.

Table 1.4: Benefits for employers and purchasers of services

- Improved quality of patient care

- Reduced staff turnover

- Appropriate use of training facilities

- Appropriate and productive use of time spent in clinical supervision

- Improved consistency and collaboration between professionals

- Increased confidence and competence for every professional in clinical practice.

(Source: Butterworth, 1995)

In a speech to the NHS Executive Conference on clinical supervision (1994) Mark Darley, Professional Officer of the UKCC, outlined the inevitability of an inter-relationship with Individual Performance Review (IPR), and stated that links with management will undoubtedly exist, but clinical supervision needs to be first and foremost between peers in clinical practice. This acceptance from the UKCC may be seen as the recognition that managerial control is not an integral part of a supervisory relationship. However the organisation may influence it's success through giving permission for it's existence, and providing the resources to make it happen.

Is clinical supervision only about clinical practice?

The short answer to this is yes. The UKCC's (1996) key statements 1 and 2 define the primary functions of clinical supervision and focus these clearly on clinical practice.

- UKCC key statement 1: Clinical supervision supports practice, enabling practitioners to *maintain and promote standards in care*

- UKCC key statement 2: Clinical supervision is a *practice focused professional relationship* involving a practitioner reflecting on practice guided by a skilled supervisor.

Does this mean that supervision is only concerned with direct clinical health care, limited to an analysis of tasks, procedures and clinical techniques? We need to consider exactly what we mean by the terms 'clinical', 'practice' and 'care'. Often we think of these in terms of actual clinical procedures and activities which we carry out. Yet we all know that truly competent practice is about more than technical expertise in carrying out nursing care. The ability to manage workloads, respond to unforeseen events, to work with others, to deliver care within environmental constraints, to balance personal and organisational goals and values in making clinical decisions are all skills which contribute to competent clinical practice. These are explored in more detail in the job competence model (Mansfield and Mitchel, 1996).

Table 1.5: The job competence model

Technical expectations

Managing contingencies

Managing different work activities

Managing the interface with the work environment.

(Source: Mansfield and Mitchel, 1996)

A more detailed explanation is as follows:

- Technical expectations: This term describes the most obvious and easily identified element of clinical practice, the specific techniques and activities which characterise the occupation. For a health visitor this might include skill in assessment of a child's development, for a nurse on a ward it could include assessment and management of wounds

- Managing contingencies: This is about adaptability and flexibility involving planning, decision making and evaluating the process of care

- Managing different work activities: No matter how skilled a practitioner is in the technical aspects of their work they will still fail to deliver truly skilled care unless they are able to manage and co-ordinate a whole range of different activities. This includes responding appropriately to conflicting demands, unforeseen events and breakdowns in systems and processes, all within the constraints of limited time and resources

- Managing the interface with the work environment: This includes all the organisational and human factors which influence how work is carried out. When delivering health care, practitioners need to be able to understand, manage and work within organisational constraints. They need to develop a capacity to work as part of a team valuing the contributions of others and resolving conflicts and barriers to effective working. An important part of this is also about recognising the human nature of work. Work is an integral part of our lives. We bring to it who we are, our values and beliefs and the effects of other aspects of our lives and take the effects and influences of our work into other parts of our lives.

How does this fit with clinical supervision? We can explore this in relation to the model suggested by Proctor (undated) in which supervision is described as having three functions:

- Formative - educational

- Restorative - supportive

- Normative - managerial or quality assurance.

The technical aspects of a nurse's work is likely to be a primary focus for the formative element of this model, particularly for new practitioners. So the recently qualified nurse starting work on a surgical ward may need to focus on reviewing and exploring practice in relation to infection control procedures, preparation for different surgical procedures and investigations, post-operative care, wound care and so on. In other words all the 'practical' aspects of nursing work which are encountered in a general surgical environment. For the more experienced surgical nurse this aspect will fall within the normative dimension of supervision. She/he has already learned and become skilled in the technical aspects of surgical nursing, so they focus in on quality and maintaining and improving standards in practice.

Managing different work activities and contingencies may fall largely into the formative element of supervision for a new practitioner. Learning to respond to emergencies, to identify priorities, manage conflicting demands and generally to ensure that all patients receive appropriate, timely care are skills which have to be learned. Supporting the process of gaining sufficient experience to make informed and clinically sound decisions in managing nursing work can help to ensure that this is a positive learning experience and that 'good' practice is reinforced and 'poor' management techniques identified and discouraged. There is also a strong restorative element here for both new and more experienced practitioners. The pressure of constantly 'juggling' conflicting demands and responding to unforeseen events on a daily basis is highly stressful. This stress can be exacerbated by uncertainty and negative feedback from patients and colleagues.

Clinical supervision offers an opportunity to explore and gain insight into the decision-making processes employed by the nurse and also to understand others' responses to these and how to manage these effectively. This leads into the element of managing the interface with the work environment which again can be a focus both for learning and support. An opportunity to 'let off steam' about difficult working conditions and relationships in a way which is directed towards developing constructive solutions.

Finally, nursing means working closely with people and building close relationships with those for whom you care. Clinical supervision provides support in recognising and dealing with the effects of these relationships . It also fulfils a kind of quality assurance function in ensuring that professional standards are maintained and the integrity of the therapeutic relationship sustained.

Table 1.6: Clinical practice and supervision

The framework of competence linked with a model of supervision can help to ensure that it remains focused on the realities of clinical practice

Nursing is a practice based profession and clinical supervision should focus on the various methods which the practitioner contributes to practice.

Is clinical supervision new ?

The idea of senior nurses directing, supporting and monitoring the work of less experienced staff has been in existence since the days of Florence Nightingale. Much of the traditional culture of nursing centred around a hierarchical structure in which clinical tasks and nursing grades were linked and the ward sister was the key person in supporting, directing and monitoring 'her' staff. Midwives have had a 'supervisor' of midwives (UKCC, 1993a) and some areas of nursing such as mental health nursing, 'client' supervision occurs. However for the majority of nursing staff there has not been a formal structure of clinical supervision as it is now being proposed within the profession (UKCC, 1996).

You could well be thinking that as nursing has existed as an established profession since the 1820's without a formal system of clinical supervision why is it appearing as such a prominent feature of the profession today? The answer is not that there is a great body of research evidence that 'proves' that clinical supervision improves nursing care and that patient care improves when clinical supervision is part of the system of care. Rather it is an acknowledgement from within the profession that the nature of nursing and the system of health care has changed particularly over the last 30 years (Fowler, 1996). These changes include:

- Task orientated systems have been replaced by a holistic and patient centred model of care

- The traditional role of the ward sister is developing into a ward manager who has increasing responsibility for finances and resource management

- Patients tend to be in hospital or under the care of community services for shorter periods of time, however during that time, patients are more dependent and in a more acute stage of their illness

- The roles that nurses are now undertaking are increasing in scope and complexity, at the same time our individual accountability is increasing

- There is recognition that the development of nursing theory needs to be embedded in and drawn out of clinical practice and is not something that can be simply learnt from or written in text books.

Nursing has changed, and is changing, building on a relationship with patients that has caring at the centre it is loosing the idea of a nurse performing routine delegated tasks within a strict hierarchy of account-ability. The nurse has a developing body of theory on which to base her/his practice and is accountable for the care given. The theory that underpins nursing is being identified, written down and researched. Although this means to some extent it can be 'taught' in the classroom, it can only be 'mastered' and developed through supervised practice. Clinical supervision is a way of taking forward some of the traditional practices of, clinical support, monitoring standards of practice and the professional development of both individuals and the theory underpinning nursing practice.

The elements that make up clinical supervision are not new, but what is new is the formal recognition that those elements are not only important, but essential to the development of nursing practice. When you think about clinical supervision try not to see it as something new, but rather as acknowledging the importance of, and safeguarding established leadership and management practices that to a large extent already exist in your clinical area.

Our area has some form of clinical supervision, does it have to change?

In most areas, some of the elements of clinical supervision are taking place. This may be very informal and staff may not recognise what is happening as clinical supervision. You may regard it as 'ordinary' peer group support. It may take the form of a chat over coffee in the staff canteen or during a quiet moment on a night shift. In most cases the 'chats' will not be planned and very often they will not have a specific predetermined outcome. But experience tells us that in the majority of cases staff feel better for having shared a problem.

Ooijen (1994) states that in order for supervision to be effective, time needs to be set aside and sessions need to last for about one and half hours. This is rarely possible during tea breaks or busy shifts, therefore systems need to be formalised and the time negotiated and managed.

If you have a system of peer support that is working

well, you may not wish to change it. However, you may first wish to ask yourself and your colleagues a number of questions:

- Do you feel supported at work?
- Do you have access to a confidential forum where you can discuss your clinical practice?
- Do you receive feedback about your clinical practice?
- Do you reflect upon your clinical practice and discuss these issues with someone more experienced?

If you answer 'no' to any of these you may wish to review and possibly develop your system of clinical supervision. By formalising the process, staff have permission to take 'time out' to discuss issues pertinent to them, however, do not be tempted to abandon a system that may have some positve points. It may be possible to build on your existing system. Firstly you need to define what it is you wish to gain from a model of clinical supervision, then how you might achieve these objectives. Any successful system of clinical supervision takes careful planning to implement and should be integrated with any work that is currently taking place in your area eg. appraisal, preceptorship, mentorship and team meetings. Existing resources may mean that it is most appropriate to adapt current support systems (Paunonen, 1991) rather than implement something new.

Table 1.7: Building on your existing system of clinical supervision

Review your existing support, teaching and monitoring process, identifying strengths and weaknesses

Do not abandon what is working well, build on existing systems

Be very clear about what it is you want from clinical supervision, identify the purpose.

Do we really need clinical supervision?

Through ambition alone you cannot reach your goal. You must have assistance from trained minds. Minds who like you craved knowledge and found it.

Hildegard Peplau (cited in O'Toole and Welt, 1994)

Peplau gained international recognition as a visionary regarding the focus and future of nursing. She focuses on what might be called the 'softer' or 'art' aspects of nursing. Much of her work has centred around the interpersonal relationships that occur within nursing practice. Even within this non-technical view of nursing she identified that nurses had a need for clinical supervision (O'Toole and Welt, 1994). She talked about a staff nurse coming to a supervisory session prepared with notes about their clinical practice. The supervisee would be expected to do most of the talking. The role of the supervisor was to perceive the interaction in the context of the situation and to suggest alternative modes of responding.

Think about your own nursing practice, to what extent do you use what might be termed, low visibility skills. Putting someone at ease, comforting them, helping them to cope with bad news, motivating them, listening to them, giving them respect, the list is almost endless. These are skills that are central to nearly all branches of nursing, yet they are not easily identified, written about, taught to junior staff or developed in experienced staff.

It is an accepted fact within the 'talking' therapies, that the person acting as the therapist or counsellor has a person that they turn to for supervision. (British Association of Counselling, 1988). This is not their own personal counselling session, but a time for them to reflect upon and discuss the progress of their client. If nursing is a profession whose practice centres around a relationship with a patient or client and if that relationship has an influence upon the persons well being, then we need some guidance, opportunity to reflect, supervision if we want to enhance our practice.

In addition to the low visibility skills of nursing, the majority of practitioners draw upon high visibility skills. This may be the technical expertise of critical care nurses working in areas such as intensive care units or haemodialysis units. Nurses working in surgical units, the community or accident and emergency areas have particular high visibility skills regarding wound care and dressings. Managing patients with unpredictable be-haviours is a high visibility skill that is common to mental health nurses. Helping someone to develop social skills is common to learning disability nurses. These high visibility skills are not restricted to particular branches of nursing and many, such as giving injections, are common to all.

As a general rule it is probably true to say that the greater the visibility of the skill then the easier it is to identify, teach and supervise. Some of these high visibility skills, once learnt, are mastered for life eg. taking a blood pressure, but if the skill involves making a professional judgement, or health technology changes, then the need for ongoing clinical supervision becomes essential.

Clinical supervision which focuses on both low and high visibility skills will enhance the clinical practice of individuals and also provide a system throughout the profession that ensures up to date and safe practice. That is an important part of clinical supervision, but it is not the only function of the process. When do you have the time and opportunity to discuss with a more experienced person an issue which is important to you? A patient discharges themselves, you feel unable to give the standard of nursing care you want to due to staff shortages, you are having problems with a student, you want to develop your career but are not sure what direction to go in. Again the list is endless, when do you have time for your own professional reflections?

Do we need clinical supervision? Nursing is a complex, highly skilled, demanding profession. Once qualified you cannot be expected and should not be allowed to 'go it alone' for the next 40 years of practice. Clinical supervision is for you, for the profession and for our patients. Can we really continue without it?

Is clinical supervision compulsory for all staff?

The position statement issued by the UKCC in April 1996 stated that,

> *Clinical supervision is not to be a statutory requirement for nurses and health visitors. This position may be reviewed if the need arises.*

However, the council is strongly supportive of its introduction into nursing as it stated that,

> *Every paractioner should have access to clinical supervision.*

Thus it creates an obligation for employers to provide that opportunity for all practitioners.

Regardless of whether clinical supervision is actually a statutory requirement there are very good grounds for nurses to pursue opportunities to develop and implement it. Nurses work closely with people in helping relationships and need to be able to take time out to reflect on what they do and how they might do it better.

Clinical supervision fits into a continuum which has developed with changing patterns of nurse education. The traditional pattern of nurse training in which the nurse served an apprenticeship and then emerged as a fully fledged and competent practitioner has been replaced by an educational process which seeks to provide the basis of a life-time of learning. Support for learning is given to the student nurse through mentorship and to the newly qualified nurse through preceptorship. Clinical supervision can help the experienced nurse develop and learn from the challenging and demanding areas of clinical practice.

This requirement for life-long learning has arisen because of the rapid changes and developments in health care which characterise nurses working lives today. Nurses need to root clinical practice in appropriate and valid research and keep abreast of new developments which can feel like very hard work at the end of a long day. Clinical supervision offers a helpful and supportive environment to explore new and current practice and to be creative in practice, taking evidence and using it imaginatively to create services which really meet clients needs. Clinical supervision is 'your time' for discussion and reflection on professional practice.

Another outcome of the increasingly dynamic pattern of health care has been an added drive for professional accountability which in itself creates a mandate for nurses to use every tool they can find to explore and question their practice. Clinical supervision promises to be a highly effective way of helping nurses to develop their skills in asking questions about what they do. In this way they are more able to accept the responsibility for their actions and to become truly accountable.

In *A Vision for the Future* (DoH, 1993) nurses are encouraged to explore and develop clinical supervision so that:

> *..it is integral through a lifetime of practice, thus enabling practitioners to accept personal responsibility for, and be accountable for, care and to keep that care under constant review.*

This is the heart of nursing. We must question, review and evaluate our practice in order to ensure that the care we give is the best for that client at that time. Although clinical supervision is not compulsory but there is a compulsion for every nurse to deliver the best care, based on the best evidence, at any given time and clinical supervision can support nurses to do just that.

Is clinical supervision the same as the supervision that students receive ?

All of us are familiar with the practice of supervising students during their clinical placements. Even if we have not had the direct experience of supervising students ourselves we have certainly been on the receiving end in our own student days. So is clinical supervision the same as the supervision of students? Although the word supervision is common to both terms, the practice in most cases is probably rather different. Consider a continuum with supervision of students at one end, preceptorship in the middle and clinical supervision at the other.

Figure 1.2: A continuum of practice

| Supervision of students | → | Preceptorship | → | Clinical supervision |

What are the characteristics of the person on the receiving end be it the student, preceptee or supervisee? The student is 'visiting' the placement, maybe for a number of weeks, but still visiting. The preceptee has just started permanent work on the area and the supervisee may have been working there for some years, with possibly many more to go. The student will have some knowledge and some experience, but this may be quite limited. The person receiving clinical supervision will probably have considerable experience in that particular area. The student will come to the area with prior conceptions which may be positive or negative. They may have a set objectives which they need to achieve for their course, these may or may not relate to any personal objectives that they may have. The students supervisor will almost certainly be more knowledgeable, more experienced and more confident regarding the placement speciality than they are. The student will thus view the supervisor as an 'expert' in comparison to their own abilities in that area. The person who is supervising the students will also be responsible for any care that the student carries out, they may also be required to formally assess the students progress and abilities.

With clinical supervision the relationship is going to be quite different. In most cases both the supervisor and the supervisee are going to be permanent members of staff. They will have an existing professional relationship which may be influenced positively or negatively by each others daily clinical practice. They will both be experienced practitioners although one will be 'more' experienced. The supervisee will have no set criteria of objectives to achieve and likewise the supervisor will have no set role on what the supervision is meant to achieve.

In some ways the supervision of a student is easier as there is a set 'pattern' to follow and set criteria to achieve. The relationship is fairly standard and from experience we know what its like to be a student. If the relationship with the student does not work out too well all is not lost as the student is only there for a few weeks. But clinical supervision is different, the 'agenda' for what is meant to happen is less well defined, the relationship is usually already established and is ongoing. Both people are experienced accountable practitioners.

Despite these differences there are a number of points that transfer from one end of the continuum to the other. White (1996) published a study which explored the supervision of P2000 students he concludes,

> *Successful facilitation was made possible through fieldwork staff who were committed to teaching students and, in all senses of the term had the capacity to do so. Such staff were knowledgeable about the educational requirements, felt ownership of the new curriculum and ensured that students were intentionally exposed to well planned learning experiences. The antithesis, however produced evidence of the barriers to good learning experience: low staffing levels poor climate and organisation of work, weak communication at all levels, staff who lacked the capacity to be motivated and felt unprepared for the student centred dimension to their job.*

Many of these words that Dr. White has used to describe successful supervision of students could probably be used to describe the successful working of either preceptorship or clinical supervision, eg. commitment, capacity, knowledgeable, ownership. Likewise phrases used to describe a system that was not working as well would be, 'low staffing', 'poor organisation', 'weak communication', or 'staff who lack the capacity to be motivated'. In a review of the literature looking at students in the clinical area Marriott (1991) identified *'good interpersonal skills as being the most important factor in promoting learning in the clinical area'*.

The practice of clinical supervision and the supervision of students are different however, there are a number of similarities and we can use our experience of supervising students to inform our practice of clinical supervision. While the idea of supervising students is an accepted part of the nursing culture and we are all comfortable and accepting of its practice, the same cannot be said for clinical supervision. Clinical supervision as an established system is new. People's expectations vary as to its purpose and function. Some may welcome its introduction, others may be suspicious. As an established culture it does not exist, it will have to be introduced into hospitals, community practices and wherever nurse work. How it is introduced will affect the way it works. Ownership by all parties involved seems to be a key feature (Fowler, 1996). Unlike supervision of students we are dealing with qualified, experienced staff who will want to focus clinical supervision in very individual ways.

What is the difference between clinical supervision and Individual Performance Review?

Individual Performance Review is an appraisal tool. Objectives are set and agreed by the manager and employee and the employees progress evaluated. The objectives set are often in line with the goals of the organisation, so that the workforce are working towards a common aim. Appraisal is driven by managers and is fundamentally a 'top down' process. The intention of appraisal is to ensure a more effective organisation (Fox, 1995).

Clinical supervision is not an appraisal tool, it is about strengthening professional identities (Paunonen, 1991). It can be used as an educational and development process and should not be used for matters relating to performance of an individual or for promotion or discipline. Clinical supervision is about support for nurses and health care practitioners, and its primary purpose is to protect patients interests (Kaberry, 1992)

Clinical supervision will improve staff performance as it empowers practitioners and enables them to plan their personal development. It will also improve competence, confidence and efficiency through the development of professional knowledge and skills. The term 'supervision' implies that the practitioners work is 'overseen' and has managerial connotations. However, the UKCC (1996) have stated that clinical supervision is not a management function, is not performance review and is not hierarchical.

In some areas the implementation of clinical supervision has been linked with the appraisal system, this ensures that clinical supervision sessions actually take place as it becomes one of the appraisee's objectives to attend. This process can raise issues of confidentiality, who is responsible for the apraisee's performance if it does not meet expectations and confusion between the role of the manager and the role of the supervisor. This confusion is emphasised when managers also act as supervisors, this is highlighted in midwifery, where appointment as a manager also entails acting as midwifery supervisor (Kargar, 1993).

Carthy (1994) describes a different type of supervision that he terms *'performance supervision'* which is based on performance management and is provided by the line manager. Performance issues are discussed by both parties, allowing the manager to give feedback. His view is that clinical supervision should be carried out in addition to performance supervision.

The authors view is that the process of individual performance review should run parallel to clinical supervision. The supervisee has the opportunity to discuss issues in either or both forums but each is a confidential setting which should not be breached by the supervisor or manager.

Clinical supervision allows the practitioner to reflect upon specific issues relating to clinical practice, to gain support regarding these issues and to develop practice based upon these discussions. It enables an individual to learn from his/her experiences without reprisal (Ooijen, 1994). Individual performance review evaluates progress against predetermined outcomes, similar to an end of year school report.

Evans (1981) defines appraisal as the:

'process during which the progress, performance, results ....of an employee are reviewed and assessed by his immediate superior; and, in many instances by other, senior managers' (p.274).

While the UKCC (1996) have stated:

Clinical supervision is not a managerial system. It is not, therefore:

- *The exercise of overt managerial responsibility or managerial supervision*
- *A system of formal individual performance review or*
- *Hierarchical in nature* (p3).

Is there a connection between clinical supervision and counselling?

The relationship between counselling and clinical supervision may be confused as some of the skills and philosophies employed during counselling may be equally appropriate in clinical supervision. It is widely acknowledged that supervision is a fundamental component of counselling and should form an integral part of any ethical code counsellors employ. Counselling is a discipline which is well defined through codes of ethics, practice and complaints, providing an opportunity for the client to work towards living in a more satisfying and resourceful way. (British Association of Counselling, 1994)

There are several factors which differentiate the discipline of counselling from that of clinical supervision. Primarily counselling generally refers to the relationship between a therapist and a client. The key word here is 'client', and clients differ from supervisees in that they enter into the relationship with a therapeutic expectation. Clinical supervision generally refers to the professional relationship between an experienced clinician and another professional (perhaps of the same discipline) who requires guidance, support, and the opportunity to reflect upon clinical practice. Supervisees have a range of professional, clinical, personal or managerial expectations. Therapeutic expectations will detract from the purpose of clinical supervision and should not feature in a relationship. Supervisors who find themselves entering into a therapeutic relationship should recognise the limitations of the role, and perhaps recommend the supervisee seeks therapeutic assistance outside of clinical supervision.

In some counselling relationships the client pays a fee and the counsellor accepts remuneration for their work. Clinical supervision usually takes place within the work context and no money is exchanged.

Table 1.8: Some similarities between clinical supervision and counselling

- The relationship is voluntarty, although each party may not have a choice of who provides the counselling/supervision or who is the recipient

- Before the relationships start, clarification is sought as the basis on which it is given, the method to be used, it's duration and confidentiality status

- The rights of the client/supervisee to make up their own mind is respected

- Counsellors/supervisors have regular appropriate supervision and support

- Counsellors/supervisors will not abuse their position of trust, either emotionally, financially, sexually or professionally

- Respect and discretion are considered vital to the development and maintainence of both counselling and clinical supervision.

Six category intervention analysis (Heron, 1990) provides a very useful example of counselling skills which may be adapted for clinical supervision. Heron identifies six ways in which a 'counsellor' can respond to a 'client'. The first three are called authoritative since in each case the supervisor is taking an explicitly assertive role which is overt and dominant in nature. The emphasis has its focus on what the supervisee is actually doing. The second set of three are called faciliative since the role of the supervisor is more discreet, the emphasis is on the effect of the intervention upon the supervisee.

Authoritative

- Prescriptive: Give advice. A prescriptive intervention is one that explicitly seeks to direct the behaviour of the client/supervisee

- Informative: Be didactic, instruct/inform interpret. An informative intervention seeks to impart new knowledge and information

- Confronting: Be challenging, give direct feedback. A confronting intervention directly challenges attitudes, beliefs or the behaviour of the supervisee.

Facilitative

- Cathartic: Release tension, encourages emotional release of tension. eg. laughter. A cathartic intervention seeks to enable the supervisee to express emotion (may be painful emotion)

- Catalytic: Be reflective, encourage self directed problem solving, elicit information from the supervisee. A catalytic intervention seeks to enable the supervisee-client to learn and develop by self direction and discovery

- Supportive: Be approving/confirming/validating. A supportive intervention promotes self esteem self-worth and value of the supervisee.

Thus there are a number of practices that can be learnt from the various models of counselling. However we must be careful that we do not try and turn a professional clinical supervision relationship into a formal counselling one. (See section on 'What do you do after saying hello?')

Is there a connection between clinical supervision and reflective practice?

Key statement two of the UKCC's position statement on clinical supervision states:

Clinical supervision is a practice — focused professional relationship involving a practitioner reflecting on practice guided by a skilled supervisor.

(UKCC, 1996)

This raises two issues. Firstly, that clinical supervision does not necessarily involve someone watching us work. Direct observation may have some use, probably for the less experienced staff, but this will be of limited value for more experienced staff. The second point to note is that, 'reflection on practice' is what the practitioner should be doing and it is the role of the supervisor to guide them in this practice.

Reflection on practice is a key part of clinical supervision, but is it not possible to reflect on practice without having a supervisor? The difficulty with reflecting upon practice on our own is that you only have your own perspective with which to view the practice.

From my own experience I find that this sort of unsupervised reflection tends to be quick, superficial and infrequent. Having a skilled supervisor adds focus to the session, prompts you to examine areas that you may not have thought about or even have avoided. In addition it allows what Hawkins and Shohet (1989,) calls a helicopter view. It is as though the supervisor takes you up in a helicopter and helps you view the situation from a greater height, thus allowing to appreciate the wider context of the situation.

Reflection on its own could stop there, but reflection as a 'tool' within clinical supervision goes further. It is the role of the supervisor not only to facilitate and guide reflection as a process of examining practice, but to encourage the practitioner to take what is learnt back into practice. As Fisher (1996) states:

While it is important to reflect on personal experience, this is of very limited value unless what is learned is applied by modifying or developing practice or seeking policy change.

Table 1.9: Reflection within clinical supervision

1.   Clinical supervision may involve direct observation of the supervisee, particularly for less experienced staff

2.   For more experienced staff, reflection on practice, guided by a skilled supervisor, is a valuable way of developing practice

3.   Clinical supervision gives reflective practice a structure in which those things which are learnt can be taken forward into clinical practice.

While it can be generally accepted that reflection has an important part to play within clinical supervision there may be people who find this approach so uncomfortable that they loose any benefits that clinical supervision has to offer them. Reflection must involve the 'self' and the willingness to be open. Snowball *et al* (1994) describe it as:

> *To engage in reflection which is maximally effective the individual needs to be minimally defensive, willing to work in collaboration with others, and be open to having theories in use tested and challenged against exposed theories.*

While this may be an ideal that all nurses should aspire to, in reality this may not be achievable. If a person is so uncomfortable with this approach they may opt out of clinical supervision rather than expose themselves in this way. Therefore we need to be flexible and imaginative in the way we introduce clinical supervision. If a supervisee feels that a particular model if being forced upon them, then they will probably react with either their physiological or psychological 'feet' and opt out. This highlights the importance of all staff being equally involved in the development and implementation of clinical supervision.

Table 1.10: Reflective practice and clinical supervision

1. There may be a degree of compatibility between reflective practice and clinical supervision

2. While this compatibilty seems justifiably high a note of caution should be introduced, reflective practice may be part of clinical supervision but it need not be the main focus

3. The strength of clinical supervision is that the model of application can and should be developed to meet the needs of groups and individuals.

Should health care assistants receive clinical supervision?

Health care assistants have a key part to play in today's health care setting. Just as the role of registered nurses varies in different branches and different settings so does the role of the health care assistant. Considerable efforts have been made in recent years to provide health care assistants with appropriate training, much of this is provided by the staff they work with and national standards have been developed with the advent of national vocational qualifications. Although the distinction between qualified and unqualified nursing staff is clearly defined the practical realities in the allocation of responsibilities and role functions between 'trained' and 'untrained' staff becomes clouded.

So should clinical supervision be part of the health care assistants working culture in the same way it is being proposed for registered nurses or should they have something different or possibly have nothing at all? Let us first make the distinction between clinical supervision and managerial supervision. Managerial supervision is the normal oversight of the daily work of the health care assistant, this would not change from the established routine of the employing authority. Clinical supervision offers an opportunity to develop clinical practice principally by reflecting upon current practice with an experienced person. While it is the professional duty of all registered nurses to take responsibility for developing their practice there is not that same professional duty for health care assistants. It may be that many health care assistants would want to make a similar commitment to their development but this is not a professional responsibility in the same way that it is for registered nurses.

The first thing to do would be to identify the need and purpose of clinical supervision for this group of staff and then tailor the system of supervision to meet the specific needs of that group. It may be that the supervision takes on a predominantly training and supportive role but this will vary according to the needs of the health care assistant. If the work of the health care assistant is so routine and free from stressful event then the value of clinical supervision may be limited, but is this really the case in today's health service?

When developing a system of clinical supervision it would probably be useful to offer one or a combination of individual supervision and group supervision. It may be that individual supervision is seen as rather threatening for the health care assistant as they may not have experienced a one to one professional relationship before.

The choice of supervisor is an important one. The obvious choice would be to link a staff nurse to the health care assistant. This may be the correct option, but again the decision should be prompted by the purpose of clinical supervision for this person. A group of four or five health care assistants meeting together once a month might provide a useful peer support network. Thus peer group supervision facilitated by the health care assistants might meet a need that qualified staff might not be able to fulfil.

Clinical supervision for health care assistants is a complex and political issue. However from the patients perspective I do not really think there is any doubt as to what the answer should be.

What is the cost of clinical supervision?

The cost of implementing clinical supervision has not been fully explored in the available literature. However if supervision is to become an integral part of every practitioner's working practice, it cannot be implemented without financial consideration and the support of Trust or employing authority.

The cost of providing supervision could be calculated in a variety of ways depending upon the exact model that is used. A simple calculation can be based upon the recommendation that every practitioner should participate in an hour of supervision every four to six weeks (Kaberry, 1992). Over a year an individual would have a minimum of twelve hours supervision, and with a one-to-one model; the supervisor would also have to commit themselves to the same amount of time. Thus for ten qualified nurses and their supervisors it is predicted that this will amount to approximately 240 hours per year.

Table 1.11: One–to–one clinical supervision

1 hour per month	Over 12 months = a minimum of 12 hours	Supervisor/s will have to contribute the same amount of time	For 10 staff = 120 hours	Inclusive of supervisor's time = a minimum of 240 hours for 10 staff per year.

If group supervision is adopted with five practitioners and a facilitator forming a group, this would amount to six hours of staff time per month. For ten qualified nurses with two facilitators, this would be equivalent to 144 hours per year.

Table 1.12: Group supervision with a facilitator

6 people (5 staff + 1 facilitator)	1 hour per month for a year = 6 hour x 12	[72 hours]	With 10 staff = 144 hours per year

Should these hours come out of the existing staff establishment, or should additional staff be brought in? This is not an easy question to give a general answer to. Resources are limited and managers will find it difficult to find 'new money'. It may be that the time for clinical supervision can be found within existing staffing establishments, but this should not be assumed, as many areas are already finding it difficult to deliver an adequate service. All the more reason to have a formalised system of clinical supervision. Each area will have to look seriously and honestly at the existing resources and current demands upon time.

The implementation of clinical supervision will beyond doubt require some investment of resources, but implementing clinical supervision may assist in reducing staff sickness and patient complaints (Tingle, 1995). If supervision does help to support nurses and alleviate stress, employers may find that they save time and financial resources that would have otherwise be spent employing bank staff.

Nurse managers should not see clinical supervision as the answer to retaining staff and saving money on recruitment costs. Clinical supervision will help to develop nurses, but if there are not opportunities where they work, they will become frustrated and move on to areas that do enable them to use and develop their skills. When implementing supervision it is important to consider opportunities and clinical career structures to ensure that the employers, as well as the individual, benefits. Clinical supervision may attract staff to a particular area if nurses are aware that there is a process of support and development which they can use. As supervision becomes more integrated into practice, areas that do not offer supervision could suffer severe staff shortages which will restrict services and result in contractual problems.

For nursing, the cost of ignoring this development may be disastrous. Clinical supervision should provide support, leadership and assist nurses in achieving greater professional autonomy. With higher expectations and fewer qualified nurses skilled practitioners will become one of the Trust's/employer's greatest investments and assets, ones which are not easily replaceable.

Managers are constantly being encouraged to use resources more effectively. To do this they must invest in individuals (Johns, 1993). If during clinical supervision practitioners are questioning their practices and allowed to examine, learn and develop new skills, *'getting it right first time'* (Deming, 1982), will be less of a problem, thus helping to attract contracts, improve quality and reduce the risk of wasting finite resources.

2

Implementing clinical supervision

Andrew Clark, Jim Dooher, John Fowler, Ann-Marie
Phillips, Rachel North and Alison Wells.

How do you develop a system of clinical supervision to meet your needs?

There does not appear to be one model of clinical supervision that is appropriate for all levels of staff and all clinical specialities. It is important to realise that there is not one 'correct' model that you have to use and possibly be restricted by. The UKCC (1996) gives a number of useful principles that you can read about in the section on: What does the UKCC say about clinical supervision? While useful lessons can be learnt by looking at the way that other areas have developed a system of clinical supervision can also be a very valuable exercise for the staff of the ward or unit to be involved in thinking through and planning how it will work in their area. It is probably not a good idea for one or two people to plan the system and then 'impose' it on other members of the team. In a small scale research study (Fowler, 1995) a number of key areas were identified which should be considered when planning the implementation of clinical supervision.

Table 2.1: Six key areas to consider when planning the impementation of clinical supervision

1. What are the various groups of staff in your ward/unit? It is quite probable that each group will have different needs and views on how they would like clinical supervision to work for them. So firstly identify the groups — **the target group**

2. What is the purpose of clinical supervision for each of these groups of staff? — **the purpose**

3. What is the criteria for the appointment as a supervisor for each of the target groups — **the supervisor**

4. What sort of relationship are you expecting between the supervisors and supervisee? What are the ground rules? — **the ground rules**

5. How much time should be spent in the process of clinical supervision? — **time involvement**

6. Does there need to be some form of formal agreement or contract regarding the process or outcomes of clinical supervision? — **an agreement.**

The target group

Different groups of staff will have different needs and expectations from clinical supervision. If a system that works well for one group of staff is imposed on another group then it is unlikely to be tailored to that groups specific needs. What are the different groups of staff in your area? There are probably qualified and unqualified staff and within each of those groups, inexperienced and experienced staff. Having identified the various target groups within your ward or unit you will then need to identify the particular needs that each of these groups have. Probably the best way to do this is to have each group to meet together and discuss what they see their needs are.

The purpose

The purpose of clinical supervision should be identified and discussed for each of the target groups. One way to do this is to examine the groups needs under three headings (Fowler, 1995; 1996a)

- Professional development which could range from a junior member of staff learning specific skills to the experienced ward sister who wants to develop research skills of finance management
- Pastoral support, which might include the discussion of difficult clinical situations or working conditions
- Assessment ranging from informal, formative feedback to formal summative assessments with quality assurance of defined standards falling somewhere in the middle.

The supervisor

The needs of the supervisee and the purpose of clinical supervision need to be matched to the qualities of potential supervisors. At the same time the supervisee needs to be able to have a say in who will be their supervisor. In some areas there may be considerable choice in who can act as supervisor, in others there may be only one or two possible supervisors. The general rule for appointment as supervisor is someone who is enthusiastic to take on the role and has the appropriate experience. A number of people may feel that they do not have the confidence, enthusiasm or time to take on another role. This is where appropriate preparation can help the potential supervisor realise that the role can be just as enriching for the supervisor as it is for the supervisee. This perspective may take a degree of 'faith' in the early stages of the relationship but the rewards of supervision should be a real motivating factor once the process is established.

The ground rules

The areas to be considered here relate to the relationship between the supervisor and supervisee, the structure of the supervisory sessions, issues of confidentiality, record keeping. It is likely that there will be some hospital guidelines for some of these issues. Again the important principle is to relate the ground rules to the purpose of clinical supervision to each particular target group. The 'contract' and 'record keeping' for a junior staff nurse is likely to be quite different to that of an experienced ward sister. However the principles may be quite similar.

Time involvement

It is important to identify the time involvement as this will help set realistic expectations for the supervisee and the supervisor. The manager, supervisor and supervisee should all agree upon the amount of time to be invested in the process. You need to identify how long and how often. Again this may vary for the different target groups. As a general guide line the more inexperienced staff will need shorter periods of supervision fairly often, maybe an hour a week. Experienced staff may require a longer session, but not as often, maybe an afternoon every month.

An agreement

The supervisor, supervisee and manager all need to be aware of and agree quite what is going to happen. If the above steps are worked through then this can form the basis of a simple agreement on what is expected of all parties involved. A major problem with the implementation of clinical supervision is that the good intentions in the planning stage never gets beyond two or three sessions because the practical issues have not been thought through and planned for. If you know that your ward gets extra busy at certain times of the year, then how will you safeguard clinical supervision time? What happens when someone moves wards, do they keep their supervisor? You cannot predict all the eventualities, but certain ones you will be able to. The agreement or contract should be used to strengthen the process of clinical supervision, not to inhibit it.

How does the ward manager go about implementing clinical supervision?

Implementing clinical supervision on a ward does not only affect the staff on that particular ward, but also nurses on other wards/directorates within the hospital/ organisation. Where the introduction of supervision is fragmented, nurses that are not in supervision are likely to view their colleagues as perhaps being in a more advantageous position than themselves. Therefore before ward managers implement supervision they must take a broader view of the organisation in which they work and discuss with their managers the overall policy regarding the implementation of clinical supervision.

The initial interest and training prior to the implementation of supervision is vital. Without this, misconceptions of clinical supervision may occur, resulting in a lack of motivation and a refusal to participate. Extensive discussions and training are essential with all practitioners to ensure that worries, problems and concerns are addressed prior to embarking (Hawkins and Shohet, 1989). Training is necessary for both the supervisor and the supervisee, thus allowing time for individuals to understand their roles, the concepts, boundaries and the skills required (Butterworth and Faugier, 1992). To neglect this initial phase could lead to lip service being paid to the whole process, with individuals and patients deriving little or no benefit. Decisions then need to be made about whether this training can be delivered 'in house' or from educators/trainers outside the organisation.

Once practitioners begin to understand the concept of supervision and are able to identify the benefits of implementing it into their working practices, there are many factors that need to be discussed. These need to address the practicalities of how, on a day-to-day basis, the supervision is to be managed in the clinical environment. Ground rules need to be established at the outset to ensure that practitioners do not become confused or despondent. It is important to consider the following questions (*Table 2.2*).

Table 2.2: Implementing clinical supervision

1.	What form of clinical supervision should be implemented and why?
2.	How should the ability of the supervisors be established?
3.	How much time have we to train and educate supervisors/supervisees?
4.	Should the supervision process be evaluated?
5.	How do we make sure that everyone does not have supervision at the same time, leaving the clinical area depleted?

The purpose and the main objective of supervision within a clinical area are important to establish (Fowler, 1996). This then needs to be supported by guidelines and standards (see *Table 2.3*) to ensure that clinical supervision has the correct focus for the nurses involved. This will also enable practitioners to incorporate the norms, values and culture that they wish to associate with their supervision.

The first session is very important. It is at this meeting that you will establish the ground rules and boundaries of the clinical supervision relationship. The author and colleagues drew up the following guidelines which are important and it will be beneficial for these to be followed at the preliminary clinical supervision meeting.

Table 2.3: Clinical supervision guidelines

a)   The first meeting may be the most difficult, as some supervisors and supervisees may not know each other particularly well. Therefore not only are you starting clinical supervision, but also a new relationship. To start the preliminary meeting it might be useful if both of you;

- Introduce yourselves
- Discuss previous professional experiences
- Speak about your professional and personal interests
- Talk about your strengths and weaknesses
- Discuss how you will both benefit from clinical supervision.

b)   It is important during the first meeting to discuss boundaries and ground rules. Confidentiality is a major issue to ensure that both of you feel safe and comfortable. It should also be remembered that incidents and occurences that affect patients must be reported in the clinical environment as stipulated in hospital standards and protocols. Incidents can only be discussed in the supervision arena after disclosure has occurred in the clinical environment. If not, action will have to be taken by the supervisor to report this incident.

c)   The idea of a learning/supervision contract needs to be explored. Issues that are discussed may involve;

- How disagreements can be handled
- Whether written records are going to be private or shared between supervisees and supervisor
- Discussing responsibility for devising and agreeing objectives and action plans for supervisees at the end of each meeting

- If supervisees wish to discuss a certain topic at their meeting, eg. quality assurance tools, does the supervisor want prior notice

- If the supervisee wishes to see the supervisor prior to their next arranged meeting, is this facility available or does the supervisor only want to have one meeting per month

- Date and time of the next meeting.

Meetings: There is a joint responsibility between supervisor and supervisee to ensure that clinical supervision meetings take place. Each meeting should be at least 45 minutes long. Whoever cancels a meeting must ensure that they arrange another date when cancelling.

Please can both parties remember that we are all very busy and if supervisees wish to see their supervisors, please can they ring first.

Once clinical supervision is integrated into the clinical area, there will still be a need for the ward manager to continue to promote and support supervision. It is important that enough emphasis and priority is given to allow nurses to leave the ward environment to ensure that they maintain the clinical supervision. Also periodic re-evaluation of supervision, the process, the purpose and the practitioner's expectations is important. Clinical supervision is not a static process and it would be misguided if managers thought that once it was in motion the process was complete when it is just the beginning.

How does a health care manager implement clinical supervision ?

As some managers of health care provision may not have a clinical background they may not immediately appreciate the need and benefits of a structured system of clinical supervision. Although somewhat paradoxically it may be the managers with the non clinical backgrounds who do value such a structured system.

Table 2.4: Twelve factors for managers to consider

1. Distinguish between managerial supervision, crisis intervention, overseeing performance, management and clinical supervision

2. Establish levels of experience and understanding within the various clinical teams

3. Identifying training needs for those to be involved through individual performance review, straw polls or staff meetings

4. Consider and monitor the time implications

5. Consider the environment for supervision to ensure interruptions are minimised

6. Ensure that all staff involved in clinical supervision feel involved in control of its development

7. Consider the use of contracts for supervision and the incorporation of clinical supervision in job descriptions

8. Recognise the importance for every team member to reflect on clinical practice within the clinical environment, as opposed to outside of it

9. Consider the implications of staff choosing their own supervisor, recognising that they may be in the best position to make this decision

10. Consider incorporating your commitment to clinical supervision in job advertisements as an attractive free bonus which promotes professional development

11. Consider the benefit to patient care and quality indicators to practice

12. Consider a standard of good practice which reflects your aspiration. Rememder, it should be specific, measurable, achievable, realistic and within a set timescale (SMART)

- Considering your outcomes (what you want to achieve)
- Considering the means by which you achieve those outcomes (how you do it)
- Considering the quantifiable things you need (time, resources, environment, system, senior management support).

Clearly some managers will not have the scope of control or resources to develop large-scale training programmes, audit and research. However that should not prevent staff at all levels within the organisation taking a structure and where appropriate 'evidence based' approach to implementation.

A one-day training event should be considered as a minimum requirement, and experience has shown that random staff selection for training, and occasional add-hoc events, are less productive (in terms of a co-ordinated implementation) than training which targets specific key staff, and teams of staff, who can cascade learning on their return to practice.

The following is an example of a standard for clinical supervision developed in the authors health care Trust.

Standard statement

Every qualified nurse in clinical practice (100%) will receive clinical supervision for at least one hour every calendar month.

Definition

Clinical supervision is a practice — focused relationship involving an individual or a group of practitioners reflecting on practice, guided by a skilled supervisor. Clinical supervision involves reflecting on practice in order to learn from experience and improve competence. An important part of the supervisor's role is to facilitate reflection and the learning process.

Table 2.5:

Structure	Process	Outcome
Each Directorate will maintain a register/list/ database of individuals who provide clinical supervision; which includes the frequency and duration of supervisory session	Each Directorate will ensure that there are designated individuals to provide clinical supervision to all qualified staff	Each qualified nurse will receive clinical supervision
Boundararies and content of the contract which includes frequency, duration,review date and anticipated content	Both supervisee and supervisor will devise a contract (or use existing format) to meet the needs of their particular requirement	A contract will exist for all clinical supervision relationships
Training session will contain definitions and key principles and process of clinical supervision	The Trust will provide (via each Directorate) a comprehensive package of learning for each qualified nurse	Every qualified nurse receives clinical supervision

(Adapted from the Leicesterhire Mental Health Service Nursing Strategy, LMHS, 1995)

Do different groups of people need to use different models of supervision?

The diversity of the nursing workforce means that there is a necessity to develop supervision in a variety of formats to meet the practitioners' needs and their different work environments. It is therefore important that practitioners read the literature and explore, debate and discuss the different models of supervision prior to deciding which model of supervision to use.

There often appears confusion over models of clinical supervision and the different methods of delivering supervision. Faugier and Butterworth (1994) in their position paper examine both of these areas. They state that models of supervision tend to fall into three categories:

- Those which describe the supervision in relation to the supervisory relationship and its main functions

- Those that describe the elements or the main function of supervision

- Developmental models which look more closely at the process of the supervisory relationship.

Probably one of the most well known models is that described by Proctor (undated). This model has three inter-relating functions which are:

- Normative: which examines the management part of practitioners' roles, it is concerned with on-going monitoring and quality

- Restorative: the supportive and helping function

- Formative: the process of skill development and the ability to reflect on experiences.

There are a variety of models that can be considered, all of which have a different focus depending upon the emphasis that the practitioners wish to place on their supervision (Hawkins and Shohet, 1991; Simms, 1993; Faugier, 1992).

A group or unit must decide what it wants to achieve from its supervision. Practitioners need to establish whether the primary function is support, professional development, personal growth or an assessment forum for learning new clinical skills. To decide what practitioners want from their supervision, small focus groups or meetings need to be arranged where practitioners can discuss what they want to achieve and the process/model they are going to implement. Once a baseline has been established, outcomes and the actual process of supervision can then be audited. Irrespective of the model which is chosen, it is important to remember that supervision encompasses many elements that interrelate and overlap. The process is dynamic and interactive and as the practitioner's needs and experience alter so may the model and method of supervision.

Table 2.6: A model of clinical supervision needs to consider these elements

- The needs of practitioner

- The purpose of clinical supervision

- The supervisor

- Time involvement

- The work context

The need of the practitioners and the purpose of clinical supervision will influence how the process is to be delivered, (Fowler, 1996). Practitioners may decide that team building and quality standards are the most important aspects that need to be addressed in their supervision, therefore they may decide to use peer group supervision. The purpose of the supervision will also help to decide whether it is delivered by managers, or whether non-managerial supervision is more appropriate. Clinical supervision is also a very personal experience (Butterworth and Faugier, 1992) and nurses need to feel at ease with how it is to be implemented.

When practitioners have decided upon the model and the mode of delivering supervision they must decide on the group from which the supervisors can be drawn. Some areas may decide to have specific criteria for individuals to be supervisors, such as a particular qualification or experience. A good supervisor is one of the crucial elements in clinical supervision. There is a danger that without adequate facilitation, individuals in group supervision may just pat each other on the back or be engulfed by negative feelings, without taking action and looking towards problem solving activities. In this instance lip service will be paid to clinical supervision, and practitioners will derive little value (Faugier and Butterworth, 1994).

Time and the work context are other elements that will affect the type or mode of supervision used. Group supervision may be an attractive proposition for some because it is seen to be less time consuming than other models (Hawkins and Shohet, 1989). Although if peer group supervision is used, there needs to be an opportunity for a group of staff to be able to leave the clinical environment together. With one-to-one supervision the overall time required is often greater, but individuals will be away from the clinical environment one at a time. This decision is obviously dependent upon activity and workload.

All staff groups are not the same and there is not a gold standard model of supervision. Getting the correct model of supervision and making it work for your clinical area is of vital importance, but it needs to have a purpose and reflect the needs and the culture of the environment in which you work. If supervision is to be developed and be of benefit to practitioners and patients, the elements that have been discussed in this extract do need to be considered.

Are there different models of clinical supervision?

One way to view different types of clinical supervision is to think about 'the structure' of how the sessions are organised. Another way of looking at the differences between different types of clinical supervision is to look at what happens during clinical supervision, 'the process'. Thus we can begin to describe structural models and process models. It is important to emphasise at this stage that there is no one model either structural or process that will meet everyone's needs all of the time. There is not a right and wrong model, what we need to do is to identify our needs and develop a model of clinical supervision which meets those needs.

Structural models

Structural models can be described as the number of individuals involved in the supervisory process and are summarised in *Table 2.6.*

Table 2.7: Stuctural models of clinical supervision

1–1:	Clinical supervision with one other
Group:	Can usually be defined as more than 3. The most common forms being a group of staff at the same level as the supervisor
Triadic or Consultative:	Three individuals, the clinical supervisor, the supervisee and one other eg. practice development nurse or clinical nurse specialist, who provides an extra dimension for the the discussion
Network:	Clinical supervision with a group of individuals with similar clinical interests

1-1 Clinical supervision

This can be provided by your line manager, a peer professional or someone who is more experienced than you. It has several advantages and is arguably the most popular model in use today. Regular contact with the same clinical supervisor, creates a good working relationship and allows the build up of trust. The trust means you will probably be more open, than for example with a group of your peers. The relationship is not compromised by the intrusion of managerial issues subsuming the clinical issues as sometimes happens if your line manager also provides you with clinical supervision.

You have the undivided attention of a more experienced practitioner to facilitate your professional development. However if you struggle to relate and find that you cannot properly engage with your clinical supervisor, you may miss out on some other aspects which other structures give you. Someone with a wider view or more than one individual viewpoint is helpful.

Group supervision

This can be useful, though is sometimes seen as a little insular. Although it may be easier to admit your weaknesses and defects in a non–threatening fashion in a 1-1 situation than in front of a group, this may particularly be the case if a number of your peer/ colleagues are present. However peers are often experiencing the same problems at the same level as the supervisee and this may make it easier to appreciate the realities of the situation.

Triadic or consultative supervision

This is useful where there are complex issues and a third perspective would be valuable. It provides a wider view than that which could arguably be achieved with only one supervisor. Someone in a management position might particularly value this sort of clinical supervision as the issues involved in their work usually have implications for a wide variety of groups of people.

Network supervision

Common interests help as problems are more easily shared, especially if the supervisee works in a relatively specialised area. However, logistically these are difficult to organise, although for some specialities this may be the only way of organising effective clinical supervision.

In practice we will often receive formal clinical supervision from one main structure with more informal supervision occurring or supplementing this in other ways.

Process models of clinical supervision

Managerial

The supervisee may value the interest that the manager takes and the commitment shown during the process of clinical supervision. However, the manager's authority to discipline may influence the supervisees willingness to share aspects of themselves they feel vulnerable about, making personal development issues tricky. Supervisees may therefore be reluctant to seek support because they fear they will be evaluated on their weaknesses. Managers may be remote from clinical issues making skills development difficult.

Peer

There may be a tendency to emphasise support (while not necessarily being able to give it because of their own competing need for it). The supervisor and supervisee may collude in not challenging each other, making personal development and standards setting difficult. One problem common to peer supervision is that individuals may feel that they have little to offer each other in terms of skills development if they are truly peers ie. at the same level. If peer systems received supervision in their turn, some of these problems can be allayed. It will be important that each has had training as supervisors and supervisees.

Non-managerial hierarchical

In setting up this type of clinical supervision the supervisor is likely to have been chosen explicitly for their supervisory and clinical skills. They are likely not to have as much authority to challenge poor standards as manager but more than a peer has. With no management problems or issues, the non-managerial supervisor is likely to be entrusted with sensitive information and feelings support therefore is likely to be well represented in this scheme.

Another perspective to the process models of clinical supervision relates to the nature of the relationship between the supervisor and supervisee.

Counselling

Specific counselling skills would be used to help the supervisee deal with difficult situations. The role of the supervisee is not to give advice or opinions but to help the supervisee understand and acknowledge their feelings. This may be very valuable following specific traumatic situations such as major incidents.

Reflection

Using a reflective model (Johns, 1996) combines a number of benefits of a counselling model but allows the supervisor to use their experience in a more directive way. It is of particular use with supervisees who have considerable experience on which to draw and reflect upon. You do not have to have a clinical supervisor to reflect on practice, but it requires considerable self discipline to sit down once a week, think about aspects of practice, ask yourself questions and to question your practice.

Proctors characteristics

Throughout this book you will see reference to Proctors (undated) three characteristics of clinical supervision:

- Formative — helping the supervisee in the development of their practice
- Normative — giving the supervisee feedback regarding the standard of their practice
- Restorative — helping the supervisee deal with the stressful situations regarding clinical practice.

Should there be a hospital or Trust model of clinical supervision?

On balance the advice would probably be against adopting a single model of supervision throughout a Trust or hospital, although if either of these were very small and providing largely the same kind of care throughout those arguments may be less applicable. While an immediately attractive idea because of the way it simplifies the preparation and training process, there are a number of reasons why one model implemented throughout a Trust, may ultimately not prove to be an effective approach.

First, we need to consider the concept of clinical supervision — what are the fundamental precepts upon which it is based?

- Clinical supervision is primarily concerned with clinical practice and therefore with patients. (King's Fund, 1994) Work with clients differs significantly from one area of practice to another and to be effective supervision must be developed in a way which is rooted in the reality of the practice area

- Clinical supervision is for practitioners (UKCC,1996). It is not a management tool or structure which can be superimposed upon clinical activity. Practitioners should therefore be encouraged and supported to take the lead in developing supervision in their practice

- Clinical supervision is ultimately concerned with developing practitioners' capacity for reflection (structured, objective analysis). (Hawkins and Shohet,1989) This should be an integral part of the whole supervisory process. It does not really make sense to present practitioners with a ready-made model of supervision and then say now start reflecting. By engaging in the process of debate and discussion about the nature of their work, what supervision can offer and how that process might work, practitioners are adopting a reflective approach from the start, which is consistent with the whole spirit of supervision.

The UKCC (1996) states:

> *The process of clinical supervision should be developed by practitioners and managers according to local circumstances. By enabling practitioners to influence the development of clinical supervision the resultant system can be trusted by all, avoiding the perception or actuality of management imposition.*

The concept of trust is another reason why it is essential to ensure local development of supervision. For the process to be meaningful trust must be established from the outset. Without this the supervisory process will be a paper exercise detracting time from other activities with little or no benefit to clinical practice.

What is important however, is to ensure that there is broad agreement across a hospital about certain key principles in supervision. (King's Fund,1994)

- The value of supervision which should ensure management endorsement of the time needed to implement and carry out supervision

- Practitioner involvement in the process

- Managers and others in authority need to sign up to the democratic principles inherent in the supervisory process (discussed above)

- Practitioners need to accept responsibility for implementing and using supervision appropriately

- Establishment of explicit agreements around the supervisory process (contracts for supervision)

- The practical decisions such as how often supervision will take place etc as well as the purpose, boundaries and so on should be agreed by all participants *prior* to commencing supervision

- Managers have a responsibility for overseeing the process to ensure adherence to such good practice.

Table 2.8: A Trust's framework for clinical supervision

Trust agreement about key principles of supervision helps to ensure that there is a framework within which practitioners can implement supervision safely and effectively. These would include:

• Commitment to the concept of supervision (recognition of its value)

• Commitment to full practitioner involvement in setting up and carrying out supervision

• Recognition of the need for supervision contracts which make agreements about how supervision is organised and supervisory boundaries quite clear to all concerned

Establishing this kind of broad agreement helps to ensure organisational commitment to the concept of clinical supervision. It also allows development of a framework for its implementation which assures the safety and effectiveness of the supervisory process, while leaving control firmly in the hands of the practitioners themselves.

What is the role of the clinical supervisor?

As with the term clinical supervision, the label 'supervisor' has connotations of management and of 'big brother', rather than an individual who can assist another practitioner with their personal and professional development (Kohner, 1994). In the author's experience the effectiveness of clinical supervision is often related to the skills of the supervisor. These skills should not be underestimated. They include listening, interpersonal skills, expertise, self awareness and unconditional positive regard (Rogers, 1957). Good counselling skills are also a prerequisite of a competent supervisor (Proctor, 1988). The role of the supervisor has been associated with that of the clinical nurse specialist or the advanced practitioner. This level of practitioner has expert clinical knowledge in their field (Butterworth and Faugier, 1993). It is proposed that all nurses who wish to be supervised will require experienced managers/ practitioners who can help them develop and examine their practices, and to enhance patient care. Supervision should be as patient focused as possible. The lists of qualities, skills and attributes of a good supervisor are endless. *Table 2.9* illustrates some of the qualities that supervisors require.

Table 2.9: Qualities of a clinical supervisor

1. Be a role model

2. Establish a safe confidential environment

3. Give clear feedback

4. Offer support

5. Analyse the good and bad moments

6. Promote skill development/challenge practice

7. Encourage personal development

8. Set standards

9. Be aware of organisational and personal constraints

10. Confront blocks

While individuals with these skills will be present in some peer groups they may not be available in sufficient numbers in others. The question really arises, are there enough practitioners to take on the supervisor's role? In the author's experience each supervisor will only be able to support, develop and educate two to three people in a one-to-one relationship or five to six people in group supervision.

However supervisors do not have to be a certain nursing grade. Some organisations may decide to have certain criteria for those individuals who wish to become supervisors, for example taking part in a supervisor's training programme, or having certain experience. Expertise and skills are important but *'supervision in the helping professions has too long been reserved for the master practitioners'* (Ivey, 1977)

It is important that supervision is integrated into the real world. There should be standards to ensure that the quality of the supervision is maintained but this needs to be realistic as nurses use many skills that are required in supervision in their daily work. As Clarkson and Gilbert (1991) state:

> *Any trainer (supervisor) requires a firm grasp of the material, sufficient experience to provide a fertile source for examples, and an on-going sensitivity to the vicissitudes of practice....clinicians who remain in the field, working with on-going challenges of their practice, are usually experienced as having greater authority as trainers than supervisors who are no longer in active practice.*

Table 2.10: Clinical supervision training

Hawkins and Shohet (1989) distinguish between five types of clinical training;

1. Courses for new first line supervisors

2. Courses for student supervisors

3. Courses in team and group supervision

4. Advanced supervision course for those who have to take a key responsibility across teams and organisation

5. Supervision courses based on the developmental model for in-depth case work

Recognising supervisors' training needs is important. Some supervisors may be very skilled, but training is still important as it allows them to practice their skills and consciously reflect upon what could have been handled differently or better. Some practitioners will choose supervisors who work in the same environment as themselves, others may decide to choose supervisors from a different discipline. Therefore supervisors' training programmes need to be multi-disciplinary. Hawkins and Shohet (1989) also discuss how training should mirror the development stage of supervision within the organisation as a whole; any training activities need to be adapted to the needs of the Trust.

Just as in all other relationships each supervision session will be different. The skill of the supervisor's role is about 'getting the best out' of your supervisee. As the supervisor becomes more aware of their role and responsibilities they will often use different styles or approaches to help their supervisee examine an issue or a problem. Ekstein and Wallenstein (1972), identify different styles of approach within the supervisors role, which include:

- Openness, of both feelings and experiences
- Self awareness, the state of being and becoming
- Reward, to give encouragement and recognition
- Generosity, in time and spirit
- Parallel process, recognising the analogy between the patient/supervisee and the supervisor/supervisee relationship.

With experience the supervisor role will develop and supervisors should become more skilled at helping and supporting other practitioners. Part of the supervisors role however, is to learn from the supervisee, the benefits of the relationship are then reciprocated so that practitioners learn more about each other, the process of supervision and patient care.

What is your role as a supervisee?

The first responsibility of the supervisee is to take an active part in the selection a suitable supervisor. You should choose someone who is honest, empathic, non-judgemental, someone who can listen and be challenging (Nicklin, 1995). Once a suitable person has been identified and they have agreed to take on the role, you must prepare for the first session.

Training will be required in the use of the supervision process, you should try to access in-house training provided by your organisation. This training and preparation should cover the skills of reflective practice and give you an understanding of the purpose and structure of clinical supervision.

You will need to identify practice you wish to discuss, be willing to share these thoughts and be open to feedback

(Marken and Payne, 1988). As you gain some experience and confidence in this relationship you will be able to discriminate between helpful and unhelpful feedback. Hopefully you should feel in control of each session as they are for your benefit. Supervisees may find it useful to keep a reflective diary as this will help to identify areas for discussion (Butcher, 1995). By writing things down it is possible to gain a deeper understanding of your actions and this will aid your learning.

If clinical supervision is implemented well then you should be involved in the preliminary discussions and you should be able to take a lead role in setting the ground rules for the sessions, thus ensuring that you feel comfortable with what is happening. If it has been agreed to keep some form of records then this should be your role. Finally you should take responsibility for booking sessions and ensuring a suitable venue is available.

During the first session you should discuss your expectations of the sessions with the supervisor to ensure that these expectations are realistic. At the start of each session you should clarify the main areas for discussion and the action plan for the following session (Cowling and Evans, 1995). You may feel rather apprehensive about the whole business of clinical supervision but remember it is for the benefit of you and your clinical practice, take the opportunity that it gives you, enter into it positively and work through any anxieties that it creates in you.

Table 2.11: The role of the supervisee

• To have an active part in selecting a supervisor

• Adequate preparation for the session

• Develop skills in reflective practice

• Identify topics for discussion

• Help set ground rules

Can you choose who will be your supervisor?

Ideally yes — but in practice there may in fact, often for very good reasons, be a limited choice. When a service is setting up clinical supervision it is logistically easier to use the existing staff resources in each area on Ward/Team. (Refer to section 'Models of clinical supervision'.) Because of this often you may start your clinical supervision career being supervised by your immediate line manager eg. your ward or team F grade if you are a Staff Nurse for instance. However there is nothing inherently wrong with this structure, indeed if you are a new member of the team you will not know the other staff members. If this is the case then it is probably better if someone else pairs you up. You should therefore make every effort to take on this role in a positive and mature way.

Here are a few guidelines:

• Do not be tempted to try and solve each others personal problems which would normally be dealt with by specialist counsellors

• Do not play games with clinical supervision it is a far too important part of your professional development and a waste of everyone's time

- Learn to get the best out of your supervisor
- Maintain a professional relationship with each other, however, if the 'chemistry' is right between you the relationship will probably develop into a true mentor type relationship. This is characterised by mutual commitment and involvement
- Do not just talk about clinical supervision — do it.

It is probably best to start with any structure rather than not to have any clinical supervision at all. As you become more experienced you will be able to identify specific areas and people that you want to be involved in clinical supervision. Remember it is as important to choose your clinical supervisor for the skills they possess and the respect you have for them.

Can the line manager be the supervisor?

There is not a clear-cut answer to this question but rather a lot of 'ifs' and 'buts'. Perhaps the most critical factor in deciding the appropriateness of a line manager being a supervisor relates to the practice focus of clinical supervision. In order to deliver effective supervision the supervisor must be able to explore practice in depth and this requires extensive and current knowledge of the practice area. The UKCC (1996) stated:

Clinical supervision is a practice-focused pro-fessional relationship involving a practitioner reflecting on practice guided by a skilled supervisor.

While Faugier and Butterworth (1992) declared:

..clinical supervision (must) focus on the supervisee's

> *behaviour as opposed to their knowledge and attitudes.*

A manager may be responsible for managing a number of different nursing disciplines. It is unlikely that she/he will share the same professional background as all the disciplines which she/he manages. Indeed in some cases managers may not have a nursing background at all. Lack of detailed knowledge of particular nursing practice or processes can make it difficult for a supervisor to provide really effective and challenging supervision. Alternatively the manager may have an appropriate background but no longer be in practice. Most managers will readily admit that it is difficult to retain a true sense of the reality of practice and to keep fully up-to-date with developments as experienced in practice.

A manager may however be able to offer an added perspective to some of the less specifically clinical aspects of nursing work. To carry out clinical care effectively nurses need to be able to work well as part of a team, to manage their work effectively and to respond appropriately to unforeseen events (Mansfield and Mitchell, 1996 — see the section 'Is clinical supervision only about clinical practice?'). In some of these other aspects of providing care the manager may be able to act more effectively as a supervisor at times than a nurse who is working within the team and may find it difficult to see beyond the here and now. One possible solution may be to develop supervisory partnerships in which a manager and experienced practitioner share the role of supervisor to a group of nurses and thereby maximise the range of skills and experience available to their supervisees.

There are other issues which need to be considered before deciding that a line manager should (or should not) be a supervisor. These are about the relationship between a manager and the practitioner(s) and about the role conflicts which need to be recognised between managerial and supervisory role (King's Fund, 1994).

Table 2.12: Potential advantages and disadvantages of a line manager being a supervisor

Advantages	Disadvantages
The practitioner (supervisee) and manager (supervisor) already have a clearly delineated professional relationship. It may be far more difficult to establish an appropriate supervisory relationship between colleagues/peers	Because the manager is also the boss it may be difficult for either the practioner (supervisee) or the manager (supervisor) to shed their habitual roles for a more open and democratic supervisory role
It may be easier for the supervisee to share difficult issues and concerns with his/her line manager than with a colleague, particularly when these are very personal or about difficulties in working relationships	It may be difficult for a practitioner to admit to concerns or weaknesses to his/her line manager because of anxieties about how this will affect the manager's view of them as a practitioner and possible repercussions eg. If applying for another job or promotion.
It may be easier for a manager to challenge a practitioner's clinical practice than for a colleague to challenge his/her peer. The pre-existing manager/practitioner relationship can be very helpful in reducing the risk of collusion (back patting syndrome)	The manager may find it difficult to establish clear boundaries between what takes place within the supervisory process and his/her management decisions. Knowledge of a practioner gained during supervision may affect those management decisions unduly or create difficulty in maintaining a management function outside supervision.

Key considerations when choosing a line manager as supervisor

- Manager's professional background
- Current involvement in practice
- Effects of manager: practitioner relationship on establishment of supervisory relationship
- Role conflicts between managerial and supervisory roles
- Confidentiality issues.

In conclusion, a line manager can become a supervisor but the above considerations need to be worked through very carefully by both potential supervisees and the manager. Managing and maintaining the boundaries of supervision in particular needs to be thought through and very explicit supervisory contracts should be drawn up to ensure that both supervisor and supervisee are clear about how potential conflicts are to be addressed.

Is there an optimum number of people that one person can supervise?

In practice it will be difficult for anyone to act as a clinical supervisor for more than three or four people. Exceptions to this may be those people who are employed with a specific role of providing supervision to other staff. If you are the nurse in charge you may feel tempted for a number of reasons to take on more staff, however consider the following points.

Key statement 4 of the UKCC's (1996) position statement states:

Every practitioner should have access to clinical supervision. Each supervisor should supervise a realistic number of practitioners.

Each supervisor should only take on this role for what he/she considers is a manageable number of people. The UKCC do not give any further advice about what a 'realistic' number may be. Clinical supervision does have resource implications, not only for the organisation but also in terms of the supervisors time and capabilities. Supervisors need to be committed to his/her supervisees and so need to decide for themselves how many supervisees he/she can cope with.

Each supervisor should act within the UKCC's *Code of Professional Conduct* (1992) which states:

> *..acknowledge any limitations in your knowledge and competence and decline any duties or responsibilities unless able to perform them in a safe and skilled manner.*

Inevitably, some areas will have a shortage of suitable people to take on the role of supervisor, good supervision can be very demanding. Supervisors may then feel under pressure to take on more supervisees, but in order to safeguard standards it is important that supervisors acknowledge his/her limitations. A shortage of supervisors can be addressed in a number of ways, for example training more supervisors, crossing professional boundaries and group supervision.

Supervision in midwifery is a statutory requirement. Midwifery supervisors are expected to supervise a maximum of forty midwives, however, she/he are only required to meet with the supervisees on an annual basis. According to Thomas (1995) midwifery supervision has developed into a system of guidance and direction rather than one of empowerment as described by much of the literature on clinical supervision (Butterworth, 1994).

Some Trusts will set standards giving supervisors

guidelines about the number of supervisees she/he should be responsible for. The desired ratio of supervisors to supervisees will generally evolve with the implementation of supervision and as each supervisor develops his/her skills.

From the authors' experience, if clinical supervision is to develop as a meaningful and useful relationship, empowering both parties rather than draining them, then an optimum of between two to four supervisees to each supervisor should be the aim.

What sort of training should supervisors have?

Laing (1965) stated:

> *There are those who have natural ability to supervise productively, and there are those who make a pigs ear out of it, no matter how many books they read or courses they go on.*

Laing's rather humorous premise promotes the idea of an inherent skill that is not influenced by exposure to an educational experience. While this may have some degree of truth, particularly in respect of the persons natural personality, there are a number of tangible skills that are utilised during the process of clinical supervision that can be, taught, developed and refined, these should be the focus of any such training.

Recommendation 11 of *Working in Partnership* (DoH, 1994) promotes the idea that clinical supervision is established as an integral part of practice up to and including the level of advanced practitioner, and it is worthwhile to consider the training implications which will be necessary to achieve this aspiration. The application of classroom theory to practice relies on a range of factors which may include the attitudes, opinions and prejudice of the supervisor, the experience and enthusiasm of both supervisor and supervisee together with the context and environment in which proposed sessions occur.

Supervisor training may take many forms, although the extent of supervisor competency will rely on understanding of the principles which underpin clinical supervision, and the actual experience of doing it. Some professionals believe that training is not necessary as they already have the skills. This may be so, but these skills should be focused through a period of preparation, and the opportunity to test preconceived ideas against training course material. For the professional who feels threatened by clinical supervision training, this will at least provide an opportunity to ventilate concerns and debate it's usefulness.

The UKCC feel that preparation that those about to undertake the role of supervisor need to address the particular requirements of the role, through a range of formal and or informal educational arrangements, adding the need for accessibility at pre– and post–registration levels. There are several principles which should be included in a supervisors' training course, these are:

- How to construct a supervision contract which defines the parameters of expectation for both supervisor and supervisee

- The ideal qualities and skills of a supervisor together with the qualities and skills of a supervisee

- Consideration of clinical, managerial, educational and personal outcomes which may be aspired to

- Understanding of what is, and is not clinical supervision, establishing its relationship with counselling, professional development, clinical competence, proficiency, performance management, managerial influences, preceptorship and mentoring

- The use of problem solving tools (such as a Forcefield Analysis) which may be used to overcome some of difficulties of implementation

- A range of supervision types, styles and models, including hierarchical, peer, group and triadic. This should include consideration of inter and intra disciplinary issues, enabling the prospective supervisor to select the most relevant and appropriate ideas for their clinical area

- How to organise a session

- Note-keeping, considering the advantages and disadvantages of recording the frequency, duration and possibly content of sessions

- Driving forces for clinical supervision from both a national and local perspective. This may include reports, local audit results, research, standards and philosophies

- The confidentiality of clinical supervision

- How to evaluate sessions and provide management with appropriate information.

These ideas may not be given enough time if compressed into a half day training event, and it is suggested that an investment in the training of prospective supervisors will pay dividends in terms of consistency, understanding, motivation, the ability to cascade information and explain concepts to supervisees, which in turn will promote the maintenance of the process, and provide a worthwhile use of time.

3

Individual sessions of clinical supervision

Andrew Clark, Jim Dooher, John Fowler, Ann-Marie Phillips and Alison Wells

What do you do after you say hello?

It is 2pm on Thursday, in one hours time you have your first clinical supervision session with your supervisee. Her name is Sally, she has been a staff nurse on your ward for the last two years. You are quite good friends and you respect her professionalism and standards of care. Although you often talk together about work you are rather unsure how to go about clinical supervision. So what do you say after you sit down and say 'hello'?

The first thing to do is to organise the place where you are meeting so that you are not disturbed, this could mean putting up engaged signs, handing your pager to someone, transferring the phone and predicting whatever else might cause an interruption. The next thing to do is organise a tea or coffee for you both. Having sorted out the privacy and comfort of the environment and a drink for you both, the next thing to think about is the content of the session. A useful framework for the content of clinical supervision has been taken from the work by Proctor (undated) who identified three areas;

1.   Formative: the developmental role of supervision

2. Normative: the on–going monitoring, evaluating and assessing role that the supervision might involve

3. Restorative: the responsibility for ensuring that the supervisee is adequately refreshed and supported.

It is a good idea to use your first session to discuss with Sally how the sessions could be structured using this formative, normative, restorative structure. In the early sessions it is useful if you include all three areas in each session, although you may want to refine this in later sessions. Fowler (1995) identified that the formative area is likely to encompass a further three sections;

- Tasks eg. interpreting cardiac rhythms

- Decisions eg. which patient do you give more time to?

- Reflective practice eg. bringing to the session a particular clinical incident.

Figure 3.1: The purpose of clinical supervision (Fowler, 1996b)

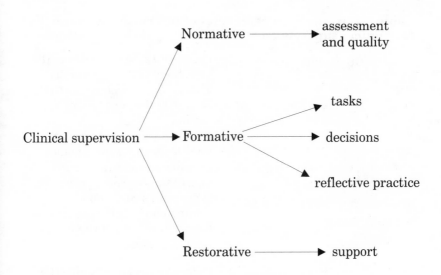

Once you have identified the purpose of clinical supervision, you are in a good position to identify what to say after you have said 'hello'. You can identify the areas that supervision will cover, eg. assessment and quality, development in the areas of certain tasks, decisions or reflective practice, and professional support. If you use these areas as a means of identifying the content to be covered during clinical supervision then the last thing you need to consider is the type of role that you take.

The work of Heron (1990) and his examination of helping relationships forms a useful guide regarding the role you take on during clinical supervision. He divides counselling type interactions into one of two classes: authoritative and faciliative. Neither of these is right or wrong but there are particular times when one or the other may be more appropriate than the other. Each of the classes is divided into three categories, making a total of six categories of possible intervention.

Table 3.1: Heron's six categories of intervention adapted for clinical supervision

Authoritative	*Prescriptive*: seeks to direct the behaviour of the supervisee. This is usually behaviour that is outside the supervisory session
	Informative: seeks to impart knowledge, information and meaning to the supervisee
	Confronting: seeks to raise the supervisee's consciousness about some limiting attitude or behaviour of which she/he is relatively unaware.
Facilitative	*Cathartic*: seeks to enable the supervisee to release painful emotion, primarily grief, fear or anger
	Catalytic: seeks to elicit self discovery, self directed living, learning and problem solving in the supervisee
	Supportive: seeks to affirm the worth and value of the supervisee's person, qualities, attitudes or actions.

(Source: Heron, 1990)

Once you become familiar with this concept then you will have six ways of taking forward the clinical supervision. Some of the direction should be thought out before the session takes place, other responses will need to be more spontaneous.

You should now be in a position to develop and take forward the clinical supervision sessions. *Table 3.2* summarises the key points

---

Table 3.2: Key points

1. Make sure that the place you meet in is private and comfortable

2. Have tea or coffee at the beginning of the session

3. Identify the content to be covered, this may include:
   - Assessment and quality
   - Development of certain tasks
   - Development of decision making
   - Development of practice via reflection
   - Professional support

4. Think through the various ways that you can handle intervention
   Authoritative:
   - Prescriptive
   - Informative
   - Confronting

   Facilitative:
   - Cathartic
   - Catalytic
   - Supportive

These ideas are not meant to be a prescriptive model on how to progress your session of clinical supervision. It may be that you take one or two of the ideas and then develop others to meet your needs. Butterworth and Faugier (1992) states that supervision is a personal as well as a professional experience and that it is this human element which allows for the variety of approaches.

Should clinical supervision sessions have an agenda?

The useful thing about an agenda is that it gives structure to the meeting and lets both people know what is happening. The disadvantage is that the agenda may control the meeting and you may rush through certain areas simply to finish 'the agenda'. If you have read the section 'What do I do after saying hello'?, you will see that there are five areas that can form the focus of clinical supervision. These can also form the basis of an agenda for an individual clinical supervision session. This may include one or a combination of the following;

- Assessment and quality
- Development of certain tasks
- Development of decision making
- Development of practice via reflection
- Professional support.

Look at the following three sample agendas, which you may be able to use or adapt to meet your situation.

Sample agenda one

Background information — you are the supervisor of Peter a staff nurse who has been qualified for two years. Supervision has been going for two months, one hour every two weeks. At the last session you and Peter agreed that this session would focus on terminal care. You suggested that Peter bring some thoughts and possibly notes to the session based on the way Peter and his team looked after Mrs Smith a lady in the last stages of her life.

- Make some coffee and put engaged notice up

- Sit down and remind Peter that the next hour is 'his' and that it is a confidential discussion

- Ask Peter if there are any specific issues that he wants to discuss today. It may be that these are discussed at the beginning or they might fit in better later on

- Ask Peter if he had managed to reflect upon Mrs Smiths care. Ask him for some feedback

- Ask him to identify areas of care that had worked well and likewise areas of care that he felt disappointed with. Discuss predisposing factors for both of these and give support where necessary

- Identify any decisions that Peter had to face and discuss how he went about making them

- Discuss with Peter the lessons that can be learnt from this and how they can be taken forward into future practice. This will not only be Peters clinical practice, but there may be lessons that the ward or you can learn

- Ask Peter if there is anything that he wanted to discuss today that is still outstanding

- Discuss the focus for the next session, identify if there is anything that Peter or you should be doing to prepare for it.

Sample agenda two

Background information — you are supervising Gwen who has been qualified for six months, but she is new to your high dependency unit. You are a staff nurse and have been qualified for two years. This is your third clinical supervision session with Gwen, they occur for one hour every week.

- Make some coffee and put engaged notice up
- Sit down and remind Gwen that the next hour is 'hers' and that it is a confidential discussion
- Ask Gwen if there are any specific issues that she wants to discuss today. It may be that these are discussed at the beginning or they might fit in better later on
- Ask Gwen to identify something about the high dependency unit that is very different from her first ward
- Give Gwen some positive feedback about how she is settling in and coping with the different environment
- Work through the appropriate section of the in-service training programme with Gwen. Relate the content of the training programme to a relevant patient on the unit. If appropriate go to the relevant patient or piece of equipment and spend time discussing it with Gwen
- Go back to room and see if there are any other areas that Gwen wishes to discuss
- Confirm details of the next session and any areas that you or Gwen need to focus upon.

Sample agenda three

Background information— you are the facilitator for a group of six ward sisters who meet together once a month for one and a half hours. The group has been going for one year and has proved to be an informative and supportive group. A basic pattern has developed over the last few months.

- You arrange seven chairs in a circle and put an engaged sign on the door

- People arrive and help themselves to a drink

- Sister Smith spends ten minutes talking about a new dressing that is being used as part of a small research study on her ward. (It was her turn to present the opening session)

- The rest of the group discuss the dressing and also the research trial that Sister Smith is heading up

- You open the discussion to explore the general issues of introducing new ideas into the ward team

- The last 30 minutes of the session focuses upon an article that the group is writing. You take a progress report and support any individuals who are finding it difficult

- You confirm the presenter of the opening session for the next group meeting and set a deadline for a draft of the article.

Most practitioners will not have a great deal of time to sit down and plan an agenda for their clinical supervision sessions. It is important however to set aside some time to at least 'collect your thoughts'. One of the roles of the supervisor is to give direction and focus to the supervisee. One of the best ways to show commitment to the relationship is to prepare for the session. The balance that needs to be maintained is that the supervisee feels an equal partner in the relationship, it is not you going in a direction that is neither relevant nor interesting to the supervisee. Your experience and knowledge should lead the direction but not dominate it. Both of you should feel that you equally control the situation and the 'agenda', if there is something more important to discuss then you should feel free to discuss it.

Is clinical supervision confidential?

Confidentiality, or more importantly, the lack of it, is one of the issues that concerns the majority of people involved in any sort of counselling or supervisory relationship. It is important to have some discussions before clinical supervision is established regarding the nature of confidentiality in the supervisory sessions. This is part of the process of establishing 'ground rules'.

Having generally discussed these and other issues, taking on board any Trust or unit guidance, then specific ground rules should be agreed during the first session. These must include the issue of confidentiality. The supervisor needs to develop a relationship with the supervisee which is based on trust and honesty, this will not be possible if the issue of confidentiality has not been agreed at the outset. Confidentiality will mean different things to different people. The British Association of Counsellors says that as a general principle supervisors should maintain confidentiality with regard to counsellors or clients, but there will be exceptions. Similar principles will also need to exist in clinical supervision.

The UKCC (1992) Code of conduct states that registered nurses must:

> *..protect all confidential information concerning patients and clients obtained in the course of professional practice and make disclosures only with consent, where required by the order of a court or where you can justify disclosure in the wider public interest.*

Any ground rule set concerning confidentiality should include some reference to the Code of Conduct and how the supervisor intends to tackle any disclosures that could potentially breach the Code.

If you as the supervisor felt that what you were discussing with your supervisee was something that you wished to take outside the session, for whatever reason, then be honest with your supervisee. Say something like, 'I do not feel comfortable handling this issue within the supervisory session, would you mind if we involved Sister Smith?'

The UKCC (1996) has said that any written records of supervisory sessions should be confidential and only released with the permission of the supervisee. However it also states, *'If clinical supervision is included in employment contracts, records may be requested by employers.'*

This raises some concerns and makes it likely that supervisees will want to keep written records of sessions to a minimum. If purchasers are asking for evidence that staff are receiving clinical supervision, it may be necessary for supervisors to record that sessions are taking place. The supervisee may wish to record the content of the discussion for his/her own benefit and for possible inclusion in his/her professional profiles.

Confidentiality may become an issue if the supervisor also has a managerial role. This situation can lead to mistrust and suspicion (Hill, 1989). This is reiterated by Kohner (1995) who states that when clinical supervision and management are linked, confidentiality and trust can be harder to maintain.

In one-to-one supervision, agreeing ground rules can be relatively straightforward, however in group supervision gaining a consensus can be more difficult. Developing trust in all members of the group can take time and this may make group supervision less effective especially at the start. This is probably one of the greater disadvantages of group supervision, not that the group will not maintain confidentiality, but it takes longer to build up that degree of trust with a group of people than with a single person. In addition with group supervision the membership may not be that constant, ideally it should be, but with the realities of clinical work, staff movement, off duty and emergencies, the formation of a consistent membership for any group is extremely difficult.

In general the issue of confidentiality is one that should not cause any problems 99 times out of a 100. As professionals we are used to dealing with confidential issues and usually we have some experience regarding the potential conflict between confidentiality and professional safety and the ethical issues that go with them. A general rule is to be honest in the relationship, if you feel it is going beyond the bounds of what you feel should be kept confidential, then say so, and discuss the issue in that way.

Should records of clinical supervision be kept?

In many cases the only record of clinical supervision will be the contract, established between supervisee and supervisor at the outset of the relationship. This will establish the frequency, duration and themes for discussion, together with review dates and evaluation time-scales.

Other records provide evidence that these aims have been met and may be divided into two main types: What happens during a session and how sessions are organised:

Table 3.2: Record Keeping

What happens during a session	**How sessions are organised**
This could take the format of:	This could take the format of:
• A reflective diary for the supervisee/supervisor completed at the end of every session	• The contract of clinical supervision
• Heading of topics discussed	• A list of dates, times and venues for clinical supervision
• A list of things that have been achieved	• A list of things to discuss eg. case load, a particular patient, education needs
• A record of feelings about professional development	• A range of skill based activities that are out of practice
• Notes about things you would discuss	• Brainstorm ideas that have occurred between session

There are advantages and disadvantages of keeping records and there may be some practitioners with good reason for concern.

Documentation which sets out to record personal and professional shortcomings alone, should be discouraged as it provides a one sided negative perspective. A question which is crucial to a clinical supervisory relationship is how confidential will discussions be and if records are kept will this alter the confidentiality of the sessions (see previous section on confidentiality). Simply, records are the property of the participating individuals and as such may not be used without permission. They may be kept within the workplace or outside it, but in both cases, thought should be given to maintaining confidentiality. It may prove useful to keep records in your professional portfolio.

What you record is entirely up to you in the context of what happens during a session, how it is used will be dictated by the decisions of both supervisee and supervisor. The confidentiality of what is discussed must recognise your organisation's need to demonstrate that clinical supervision time is being used constructively. This may take the form of providing information for audit. Generally audit tools which question the content of sessions focus on themes rather than what is actually said and again, what you disclose is up to you.

Records provide a useful bridge over the space between sessions, enabling participants to easily refer back to a topic or issue from preceding sessions. In a one-to-one relationship it is usually the supervisee that keeps the records and the recording process will be quite simple. For group supervision there may be a designated note keeper or all participants may keep their own notes.

Clearly the right to safety for both supervisee and supervisor would be placed in jeopardy if either party felt records of sessions would be used as evidence to incriminate a participant (Butterworth, 1995).

How much time should be allocated for clinical supervision?

Time or lack of it will undoubtedly be one of the main obstacles to the successful implementation of clinical supervision. A common standard is that each supervisee receives on average at least one hour per month.

Let us consider how a supervisor with four supervisees can creatively organise and make the best use of time. We will assume that supervisees and supervisor work 37½ hours per week and 4 weeks in a month, collectively they have 750 hours working time.

One-to-one:

- Here the supervisor devotes one hour to each supervisee per month
- A total of eight hours is given to supervision; four hours by the supervisor and one hour each by the supervisees.

Group:

- Here the supervisor holds a 1½ hour group session attended by all four supervisees.
- A total of 7½ hours has been given to supervision, 1½ hours each by the supervisor and supervisee
- The supervisor has gained 30 minutes.

One-to-one plus:

- Here the supervisor holds individual sessions for each supervisee lasting 45 minutes once per month.
- In the same month the supervisor holds an additional session for one of the supervisees lasting one hour.(This may be tagged on to the original 45 minutes or held separately, and will alternate between supervisees)
- A total of eight hours has been given to supervision and participants will benefit from regular individual time.

One-to-one and group:

- Here the supervisor holds individual sessions for each supervisee lasting 30 minutes once per month

- In the same month the supervisor holds a session for all four supervisees lasting 45 minutes

- A total of 7 ¾ hours has been given to supervision and participants will benefit from individual time and group time.

Group and one-to-one

- Here the supervisor holds one hour group sessions attended by all four supervisees

- A total of five hours has been given to supervision. The agreed standard allows for eight hours and one way to use the extra time may be to;

  undertake the clinical work of a supervisee for one hour

  then hold a one-to-one supervision session lasting one hour to discuss aspects of clinical work for that supervisee;

  rotate this process including all four supervisees to achieve group supervision every month for all, and individual supervision for one person every week.

- This enables the supervisor to have a real knowledge of the supervisees' workload to bring greater understanding to the one-to-one session. It also demonstrates a direct benefit to patient care in having the advantage of being able to draw upon a broader range of clinical experience.

- A total of eight hours has been given to supervision and participants benefit from group supervision and rotating individual supervision every month.

There are many creative solutions to the obstacle of time for supervision, although when considered in numbers of working hours per month the participants are devoting about 1% of their time. One hour per month should be considered a minimum and, in many situations, more time could be justified. The examples given have not taken into account the training necessary to establish good practice and this should be taken into account to ensure adequate preparation for both supervisee and supervisor. The calculations do not account for the time the supervisor spends receiving their own supervision.

Remember to ring-fence your clinical supervision time as there will be many other competing priorities, all of which may be the reason for not getting started or adhering to your plan.

What does it feel like to be supervised?

Clinical supervision is like anything other relationship, sometimes people feel an almost instant warmth and attraction, alternatively the opposite can occur, usually it is somewhere in between. So if it is not instantly wonderful do not worry. Persevere with it as you and your supervisor need time to grow together. If you have a good supervisor you will feel restored, facilitated and developed. You will also feel challenged and motivated. Remember, supervision like any other relationship requires commitment from both parties, do not expect the other person to supply the motivation or be in charge, this is a professional relationship between adults. As a supervisee do not be tempted to slip into a passive, child like role or play some sort of control games. Treat each other as adults and respect each others personal and professional experience.

Unfortunately it sometimes happens that people initially have negative experiences of clinical supervision. If this happens, try to see if there is any extra clinical supervision training that you and/or your clinical supervisor can access. It is worth persevering with your clinical supervisor, be honest with them and discuss your expectations of clinical supervision. Try to actively seek help from someone who is having successful clinical supervision and adapt the approaches that they find successful into your own experience. Alternatively and as a last resort, if it proves impossible to engage in meaningful dialogue, then it should be possible to change clinical supervisors.

Different people will have different experiences of clinical supervision. In the same way that you will get different answers when you ask a number of people what does it feel like to be married? You will get different answers when asking a similar question to people being supervised. Our response to this sort of question will depend upon a number of factors eg. our previous experience of being supervised, our clinical experience, who is supervising us, what type of clinical area we work in, what sort of personality we have, how we view authority figures, whether we have just been promoted, or whether we have just been turned down for a job.

Most people will feel a little apprehensive if this is there first experience of clinical supervision. This is true of the supervisors as well as the supervisees. The situation for most of us is quite new. Although we will have had assessors and supervisors as part of our training, clinical supervision is different, but until we get into it we do not really know how different or what is expected of us, is this a management tool? That is principally why this book was written in the way that it is. Some people find clinical supervision a 'wonderful' experience, and talk about it with an almost charismatic zeal. Others dismiss it as a waste of time. These are probably the two extremes with most peoples experience falling somewhere in between. A number of external factors will affect our experience of clinical supervision e.g. what degree of influence we had in the initial discussions, could we choose our supervisor, is the time safeguarded, do we feel that the supervisor is fitting us in? However probably the most important factor that will influence our response to clinical supervision is our own motivation and personality. Are we prepared to put something into this relationship? In the realities of the work environment this is not always easy, when we are short of staff, feel used by the management, undervalued by our colleagues etc these are feeling that most of us have at some time. But the nature of being a professional means that we must acknowledge and then constructively deal with these feelings, rather than let them fester. If we are prepared to use clinical supervision in an honest and adult way then the experience will be a positive, although at time possibly an uncomfortable one.

What does it feel like to be a clinical supervisor?

The clinical area in which I work has been developing and implementing clinical supervision for the last eighteen months. Initially there were four supervisors for ten qualified nurses, one-to-one non-managerial supervision was used. The following are thoughts and reflections of those supervisors involved.

The quality of the relationship is as important to the supervisor as the supervisee. The supervisor wants to develop, support and educate the practitioner. Hopefully during supervision the supervisor can effectively put the necessary skills into practice to help the supervisee reflect and learn from their own experiences. Thus steering away from traditional hierarchical relationships where the more experienced practitioner has a tendency to take over or problem solve for the other (Munroe, 1988). A supervisor, just as any individual who enters a new relationship, wants to gain and learn from that relationship. One supervisor when describing their thoughts on the supervision process stated that:

> *To be effective, sessions need to be thought out and reflected upon, both from the point of view of what is happening within the session and what is happening personally. How am I performing as a supervisor? How could I be better? What have I learnt about my supervisee? And what have I learnt about myself?*

These are all important questions for the supervisor to ask as they have implications for their own development and for the success of future supervision sessions. Although all the supervisors were experienced nurses, each felt a little unsure of themselves when they first agreed to become a supervisor. Being a supervisor is a demanding role and it is likely that they themselves will need a support group where confidentiality is not breached, but where the supervisor can generally discuss issues or concerns.

Establishing the ground rules and acknowledging what can and cannot be offered is just as important to the supervisor as the supervisee. For instance it needs to be decided if supervision can be immediate, if the supervisee feels that there is an issue that cannot wait for the next scheduled supervision meeting. Some supervisors, because of other commitments, may only be able to provide an hour's supervision per month, others may have more flexibility. It is important that supervisors are aware of the commitment and that by supporting this development, space has to be made in their already busy diary, *'Clinical supervision necessitates an investment in commitment and time'*.

Supervisors who supervise two or three individuals are likely to find that some relationships are easier than others. As a supervisor it is likely that you will be motivated more by some supervisees than others. Being able to understand this and still have an open, honest relationship that can help the practitioner, can be difficult. Supervisors like supervisees need to recognise when a relationship within the supervision process has problems. How this situation would be handled needs to be discussed, with the ground rules, in the first supervision session. It should also be remembered that supervisors do have bad days too and are not infalible.

While the supervisor's role is not an easy one, in the author's experience supervisors gain from the satisfaction that they are contributing to and discussing nursing care, thus they were allowed *' to influence practice in a positive way'*.

Suppose you do not get on with your supervisor/supervisee?

It is important that when you choose a supervisor or agree to be a supervisor that you do so carefully. You may find it difficult (although not impossible) to opt out of the relationship once it is established. If you choose the right person (whichever role you are in) it can be a highly successful partnership. An obligation to receive or to give supervision may be included in your job description, it is important that you do not get involved in an unproductive.

You need to ensure you have a means to dissolve the partnership.

At the first session you should agree ground rules, one of which should be that if either party wishes to bring the relationship to a close that it is acceptable to do so. Supervision partnerships will evolve and change in time and supervisees will 'outgrow' his/her supervisor and neither party should take this personally.

Inskipp and Proctor (1995) identify a number of 'indicators' for changing your supervisor, these include:

- Reaching a new stage of professional and/or personal development
- A change of client group
- A change of job
- Developing collusion
- Becoming aware of a 'mismatch'.

Inskipp and Proctor (1995) suggest the time to discuss these issues is at a review session and that the supervisee should let the supervisor know so that she/he can prepare for the session. As this will be the ending of a professional and possibly, personal relationship, the supervisee should ask for some final feedback.

As a supervisor you may agree to supervise someone who needs more support than you had anticipated. Peoples changing needs cannot be predicted. If you feel you cannot support the supervisee in a way he/she will benefit, then you have a responsibility to be honest with yourself and the supervisee. Neither of you will benefit from this type of situation. You may wish to help the supervisee choose someone else, so that she/he are not left unsupervised.

Table 3.4: Choosing a supervisor — a checklist

	Yes	No

Is the person:
The right age?
The right sex?
The right ethnic background?

Does she/he have:
The right skills
Relevant specialist expertise?

What are my needs at the moment?
clinical
managerial
professional

Do I want someone who works in my area?

Who meets this criteria?

Who might be able to recommend the right person?

4

Working examples

Andrew Clarke, Jim Dooher, John Fowler,Chris Hale, Kim Jacobs, Ann-Marie Phillips, Rachel North and Alison Wells

How could it work for a staff nurse working in mental health?

Clinical supervision can work especially well for staff nurses working in mental health because the range of potential supervisors is quite large; the F and G grades, managers, practice development nurses, clinical nurse specialists and peers.

Staff nurses have a direct role to play in the delivery of health care, often functioning as key workers both within the traditional institutions, community homes and in the patients own homes. It is therefore vital that staff nurses, regardless of where they work, receive good quality clinical supervision. They are often responsible for the day to day decisions of care, and this often is at a time where more senior staff are absent eg. evenings, nights, weekends. To be fully effective the whole mental health team require clinical supervision, but within the team it is probably essential that the staff nurses need good support and clinical supervision from more senior colleagues.

A newly qualified staff nurse will have many expectations surrounding the change from student to staff nurse and the responsibilities within the multidisciplinary team. A new graduate needs time to learn, process, make mistakes, see successes and continue the learning process

(Gadell, 1986) Although all student nurses are 'supervised' during their training this is mostly focused on completing appropriate objectives required by the university. Receiving clinical supervision in the capacity as a staff nurse has a much wider focus (see section on 'Is clinical supervision the same as the supervision that students receive?').

Initially newly qualified staff nurses may have a mixture of 'ideals' of quality patient care and a number of fears and reservations regarding working as a qualified member of the team. Receiving the support and direction from an experienced nurse in the clinical supervision setting allows staff to examine the ideals of practice and their application to practice, and to build up their confidence and experience. The reflection on practice can lead to more realistic goals and help with the post euphoria dip experienced by many newly qualified staff as they enter the workplace on a full time basis. Discussing the constraints of resources and their implications for practice in a formal environment enables both newly qualified and experienced staff to explore various approaches and solutions, which at first may not appear obvious.

The more experienced staff nurse will appreciate the opportunity to sit down and discuss pertinent issues with a more experienced member of staff. It is these staff that are often overlooked, they are experienced members of the team and work in a competent manner and can be relied on when the team is busy. However as team leaders we may overlook their need for support, guidance and feedback on their work, more importantly we may not give them time for themselves.

It is important for everyone to realise that even very experienced staff do not have all the answers and the clinical supervisor is not meant to be some sort of all knowing being. However, experience wisely used, can provide the basis for encouragement, reflection and viewing a situation from an objective perspective. Clinical supervision may highlight strengths but also areas where improvement is needed. This may feel somewhat negative but it should be honestly examined and if appropriate be seen as a proactive step towards lifelong learning and development.

> *Staff nurses are at the very sharp end of intervention and require regular quality supervision. It is essential to establish a culture of care for staff.*

(Davies 1993)

How could it work for a ward manager on a medical ward?

Most clinical leaders/ward managers would agree that often they do not have as much time as they would like for staff development and in depth discussion with practitioners about their individual case loads. Clinical supervision enables this to happen in a systematic and structured way. Implementing clinical supervision in a ward, unit or a community environment is time consuming and requires a great deal of commitment from the clinical leader. This is an important development for nurses and there are a variety of issues that ward managers have to address, so adequate preparation time is vital. Some issues for the ward manager to address include:

- What form should clinical supervision take and why?

- Who could and would be supervisors?

- How often would supervision occur and how feasible is this?

- How would the supervision process be evidenced?
- What kind of training programme is required?
- How could the ability of the supervisors be assessed?

As with all changes it is necessary for ward managers to discuss with their staff the reasons why they think clinical supervision is important and how it may benefit practice. This includes discussing supervision at ward meetings, having debates and reading literature. The qualified staff that work on the author's medical ward, decided that they wanted to implement one–to–one non-managerial supervision. The practicalities of how supervision would fit into the day–to–day routine of practitioners is important and was established before supervision started. Simple solutions such as supervision sessions being marked on the off-duty rota, with only one nurse at supervision at any one time are important house rules. Everyone going to supervision on a Thursday afternoon is a ward managers nightmare.

As a manager it is important to recognise when embarking on supervision that your staff may be influenced by a supervisor who could be from outside of your practice environment. This is healthy and necessary, but visions of ten qualified staff all trying to implement change at the same time did cross the author's mind, although in practice this was never a problem. The management of change is however important to consider, as supervision will hopefully encourage staff to examine their care and change practices. The motivation of individuals who were attending supervision did increase and suggestions for improvements were numerous and very welcome. Clinical managers must realise that if their staff are to participate in supervision, this challenging and open environment must also be reflected in the clinical setting.

The most difficult time for the ward manager is at the beginning of supervision. Mainly because you (the ward manager) have invested a great deal of time in preparation and training. Feedback from the staff does not initially occur, so you are left wondering whether everything is going to plan. This period is understandable as the supervision relationships are young and also the nurses are testing the ground rules and the confidentiality aspect of the process. In the author's experience staff do not discuss their supervision outside the sessions until about four to five months into this process. As practitioners gain more confidence some of them begin to discuss ideas or situations which they had previously discussed with their supervisor.

Managers must also consider the differences between appraisal and supervision and how the two should be managed (see section on 'What is the difference between clinical supervision and individual performance review?'). While both these processes may be carried out by the same person, it may be difficult for the manager/supervisor not to be affected by what happens in both arenas, and conflicts between the two roles are likely to occur (Hawkins and Shohet, 1989). Supervision should be linked to support and professional development and not pay and reward (Kohner, 1994). If this separation does not occur it is likely that nurses will not feel that their supervision is taking place in a 'safe' environment and they may opt out of this process.

Many nurse managers would agree that nurses in today's health care environment are continually being asked to learn new clinical skills and take more and more responsibility. The importance of utilising these and other decision making skills are important for practitioners as clinical managers are not always present in a 24 hour service. Clinical supervision is one process that could be used to help to increase professional autonomy and aid the development of expert practitioners.

While there is the necessity for more research to establish a link between clinical supervision and patient outcomes, quality of care is high on all ward managers' agendas. Supervision could be incorporated into the manager's quality and audit plans. As long as the supervision process has been standardised, training has been extensive and appropriate supervisors have been utilised, this 'bottom up' approach to quality can be driven by practitioners discussing and examining their care, which appears to be a realistic way of improving quality.

If supervision does reduce complaints (Tingle, 1995) and sickness, this will reduce the time that clinical managers have to spend answering complaints and trying to employ bank staff. In the author's opinion, the long term benefit will outweigh the cost of training and implementing supervision.

How could it work for a district nurse?

One of the most important decisions to make when implementing clinical supervision is 'how'. This may seem very obvious but it is the most important decision as to whether implementation will be successful. Certain key principles, illustrated in *Table 4.1*, need to be applied when making this decision.

Table 4.1: Implementing clinical supervision for district nurses

Everyone should be clear about the purpose or aims of supervision

All those who will be involved should participate in the discussions about how to make supervision work

The team characteristics should be considered — size; different grades and experience; specialist knowledge and skills etc.

The pattern and nature of work should be explored — how it is organised; where the stresses are; new demands and skill requirements; type of client populations etc.

When thinking about the last two points you will probably find that certain things stand out as specific to district nursing. These might include:

- Team organisation — district nurses are commonly organised into teams which comprise different nursing grades and will probably have a wide range of experience within the team

- Practically based and with clear outcomes — there is a strong practical focus in district nursing work and much of it is amenable to clear outcome measurement as a demonstration of clinical effectiveness, for example the healing time of leg ulcers or effective pain management. These are readily scrutinised and factors influencing choice of interventions can be explored.

- Elements of specialist expertise — a number of areas of district nursing work may include some specialist skills such as those concerned with tissue viability, continence management, care of Hickman lines etc. It can be helpful to access specialist nurses to support scrutiny of care in these areas.

- Clients with special needs — district nurses work with such a wide range of people with such varied needs that this could apply to all their clients. However, there is no doubt that some client groups may present greater challenges and demands than others. Perhaps the most obvious example are people who are chronically or terminally ill. Unlike in the acute hospital where long-term care is generally measured in weeks, district nurses may care for people over months or even years. The restorative function of clinical supervision has a crucial role in supporting nurses in managing such close, caring relationships and the attendant loss if their patients die.

Table 4.2: Key points

Team organisation

Practical work with clear outcomes

Areas of specialist expertise

Working with clients with special needs and over long periods of time

This kind of understanding about what is 'special' about district nursing should be considered alongside the types and methods of supervision which are available to find the best fit. There are a lot of different models of supervision which often describe supervision from different stand-points. They may focus on the purpose or functions of supervision, eg. Proctor's (undated) three function interactive model which identifies three 'interlocking' functions of supervision:

- Formative - or a learning process
- Restorative - or support
- Normative - or managerial/quality control.

Alternatively they may focus on the characteristics of the supervisory relationship. eg. Frankham's (1987) '12-role model of supervisor functions' (*Table 4.3*).

Table 4.3: Frankham's 12–role model of supervisor function

Monitor	Professional representation	Mentor
Manager	Teacher	Mirror
Evaluator	Analyst	Facilitator
Reviewer	Trainer	Therapist

Again, others have focused on the supervisory process itself. These are derived principally from counselling and psychotherapy but may have much to offer nurses who work very closely with clients and families over fairly long periods of time as may often happen in district nursing. Hawkins and Shohet's two matrix model of supervision explores particular client interventions and nursing processes and also what occurs during the supervision process and how this can further enlighten understanding of nurse/client interactions (Hawkins and Shohet, 1989).

Although these models are presented separately all these aspects of supervision need to be considered when making that final crucial decision about how supervision will be delivered. There are a wide range of options (*Table 4.4*) but some will feel more natural to your particular conditions and needs.

Table 4.4: Models of delivery of clinical supervision for district nurses

One–to–one with a more experienced (higher grade) district nurse acting as supervisor to a fellow district nurse

One–to–one with a supervisor from a different discipline

One–to–one with two district nurses of the same grade

Group supervision which may be:

- Peer groups within the team
- Peer groups across two or more teams
- Groups supervised by a more experienced supervisor eg. district nursing sisters supervising a group of staff nurses
- Team supervision involving the whole district nursing team
- Team supervision involving all or part of the multi-disciplinary team

Network supervision that provides occasional external input into any of the above eg. accessing nurses from a different team to explore particular areas of practice or using specialist nurses to provide supervision for areas of 'specialist' practice. (Faugier, 1992)

So how can you decide which would be best for you? Here are a few examples of what can work for different groups.

- Large team with a number of relatively junior, inexperienced staff — senior nurses within the team take on a supervisory role with a number of junior nurses. This may be one to one or group or a combination of the two.

- Small experienced team working closely with other members of the primary health care team — multi-disciplinary team supervision

- Large experienced team — may divide into two or more smaller teams for a modified form of team supervision. Alternatively could develop peer group supervision within the team.

Other issues to consider include:

- Time and other practical constraints — group supervision involves significantly less time out across the whole team. Particularly where there are relatively few potential supervisors this may be a much more realistic option than one–to–one supervision. Availability of rooms and fixed commitments like clinics need to be considered when deciding who should supervise whom and where

- Number of highly dependent clients or those requiring complex or high levels of intervention — group or team supervision which focuses specifically on the nurse, client interactions, interventions and processes involved in the care of these clients may be supported by an external supervisor, eg. a specialist nurse, MacMillan nurse etc. In addition, group supervision may be supplemented by one–to–one supervision for those nurses most involved in the care to ensure that the learning opportunities are realised and the nurse is supported and helped to work through the effects of his/her involvement with the client

- Looking at specific interventions or nursing processes — it may be helpful to access specialists from within the team, from the wider multi-disciplinary team or other specialist nurses to act as supervisors when helping the team or groups within the team to explore particular areas of practice, eg. pain management; continence management, assessment and care of clients who are nutritionally at risk and so on.

There really is no limit to the possibilities so be prepared to experiment. Clinical supervision is an endlessly adaptable tool which can help you to explain, analyse and reflect on the way in which you practice to promote standards in care. The term 'horses for courses' is worth keeping in mind when you're trying to work out how to implement it successfully. You do not need to be tied down to a single approach. So long as you are clear about what you want to achieve be inventive and imaginative in finding the best way to get there.

How could it work for a staff nurse in a learning disability group home?

John qualified as a staff nurse three years ago. For his first two years he worked on a busy challenging behaviour ward. He enjoyed the work on the ward but wanted to gain experience in a different setting. When a staff nurse post was advertised in a community group home he applied and was very pleased to have been offered the job. During the interview the nurse in charge of the home said that John would have a clinical supervisor. John had not had clinical supervision in the challenging behaviour ward and despite making enthusiastic comments during the interview he was somewhat unsure as to how it would all work. A year on he reflects upon the experience.

> When I first started at the home I was rather unsure of myself, on the challenging behaviour ward I new what I was doing. The work was hard and very demanding but I enjoyed the pace and the demands of the ward. When I moved to the home it was almost like starting again. The work was completely different and I was often working on my own in charge of the home. Despite having some reservations regarding clinical supervision I soon realised that it was not something that I had to

do but it was my time, it was for me. Sally was my supervisor, she was an F grade and had worked at the home for the three years since it opened. We met together for one hour every two weeks. The time for clinical supervision was built into the off duty and we met in the study room at the home. Sally put an engaged notice on the door and we had a coffee while we talked.

During the first session Sally asked me about the challenging behaviour ward and the role that I had there. We discussed the differences in the work and how I was settling in to the home. During the first few meetings we developed quite a lot of trust, both me of Sally and Sally of me. After a while a pattern developed, I tended to do most of the talking with Sally asking some key questions and giving me feedback and at times advice. Initially Sally got me to identify what I felt my needs were and then we discussed these. She suggested that I keep a brief diary of important happenings in the home. This proved much harder than she or I imagined. I managed to keep a few notes which tended to be a couple of sentences such as 'Fred would not get out of bed this morning, I tried to talk to him and persuade him but he would not move, gave up but was unsure if he was playing games with me, or if he genuinely did not want to get up.'Sometimes we would just discuss one of these incidents, other times we might cover a number of issues.

Clinical supervision has been going for about a year now and I have found it very valuable. If Sally is on annual leave I really notice the difference. If something happens during work I know that I will be able to discuss it with Sally at the end of the fortnight. There is a new health care assistant starting at the home next week and I will be her clinical supervisor. I'm really looking forward to this and although I have looked after students and new staff on the challenging behaviour ward I never really felt the enthusiasm that I now feel.

Working with Sally over the last year has given me a different perspective on supervision. If I had to sum up the experience I would say, 'it is my time.'

How could it work for health care assistants?

The role of the health care assistant (HCA) has developed greatly over the last few years in relation to the role that was undertaken by nursing auxillaries (Dewar and Clark, 1992). Indeed the distinction between trained and untrained staff is in some areas becoming blurred. Some HCAs working in the community setting are responsible via registered nurses for their own caseloads. Others especially those with NVQ qualifications (or equivalent experience) function at quite responsible levels often working in a relatively unsupervised capacity, and may work for long periods on their own. (See section 'Should health care assistants receive clinical supervision?').

Arguably HCAs fulfilling these and other roles are as entitled as registered nurses to receive high quality clinical supervision. This will be particularly relevant when they are working in the community or have delegated responsibility.

When considering who will be the supervisor similar considerations should be taken into account as with the rest of the health care team. A degree of choice is essential, someone who is a more experienced practitioner and has a keenness to take on the role. A junior D grade may not be a good choice, although a registered nurse they may have limited experience in that setting.

Where an HCA is being clinical supervised by an E grade staff nurse the following structure is suggested in *Figure 4.1.*

Figure 4.1

$$G/F \longrightarrow E \longrightarrow HCA$$

It is also suggested that periodically the G/F supervising the E grade
sits in on the clinical supervision of the health care assistant

Experience with health care assistants working in
community settings suggests that clinical supervision
works well in community teams using peer support and
supervision groups which combine all grades of staff. Staff
working in a nursing home or similar situation where
there is a high ratio of HCAs to each registered nurse will
find the practicalities of introducing clinical supervision
very challenging. Ironically it is in these situations where
the elements of clinical supervision (support, monitoring
and development) are crucial in the delivery of high quality
care that the implementation is likely to be the most
problematic. (See the section on 'How it could work for
someone working in a nursing home?' for a more detailed
discussion of the issues involved.)

Health care assistants tend to be the last group to
receive clinical supervision. Although it could be argued
that their needs are as great if not greater than registered
nurses. This is particularly true for those staff working
in the community often spending a good deal of the time
on their own. Throughout training registered nurses
experience and become familiar and comfortable with
the general concept of 'being supervised'. For some
HCAs this may be a new experience and one they do not
feel comfortable with. Some staff may initially find the
thought of supervision stressful however with skilled
supervision from a sensitive supervisor and comments
like 'I don't know how I survived without it' these are
eased.

It can be hard for health care assistants whose training needs are often neglected by some organisations to understand the reason behind the drive towards clinical supervision. However the pressure of work of many staff is helped by regular access to clinical supervision, with a list of issues to take to supervisors at regular designated intervals, often preventing the need to bother qualified colleagues with every query at the time they arise. One HCA commented that 'at first you do not always realise that you need it, but after a while you realise that you do and that you wonder sometimes just how you survived all those years without it.'

How could it work for a clinical nurse specialist?

A common complaint by clinical nurse specialists and other senior clinical nurses 'who is there to supervise me?' or 'where do I unload my work stress within the work environment?'. Clearly at this level opportunities to relate to 'more experienced' staff are limited. However there may be other senior staff in different specialities but with similar issues to discuss. Peer group supervision with other specialists in the same area may be a possibility, also it is worth considering staff with greater specialist knowledge, but they may not be nurses. The important thing to consider at the onset is what is it you want out of clinical supervision and then consider who the appropriate supervisor or combination of supervisors could be. Suggestions may include:

- One–to–one with peer (inter trust clinical nurse specialist - clinical nurse specialist)
- One–to–one with peer (own trust clinical nurse specialist - clinical nurse specialist)

- Group with peers (own trust clinical nurse specialists)

- 1-1 with peer and an other clinical supervisor (triadic)

- Use of other disciplines

- Network approach where several individuals with common interests gather for clinical supervision

- Senior trust nursing staff (non clinical) staff.

Little work appears on who supervises the most senior practitioners, but it would appear to be most logical that clinical supervision on a one–to–one peer basis would work well for senior practitioners particularly in respect of their clinical component. As with other practitioners it may be logical for different parts of their role to be supervised by different people, thus separating out the clinical component from their organisational and development and managerial roles. Opportunities may arise for both inter– and intradisciplinary clinical supervision at this level, which may be within or outside of your organisation. Indeed some authors recommend the use of other professionals (Platt–Koch, 1986).

Although at first sight the idea of one–to–one peer supervision within an organisation or outside it at this level may appear impractical, this in fact is not the case. There are several advantages. The internal market however discourages the wider dissemination of good practice, though this may change if the policy is amended. There is also the perception of the potential to breach confidentiality if clinical information is taken outside of the Trust. In reality this should not be a problem as all NHS staff are bound to adhere to the same level of confidentiality. There are disadvantages of using an outside link for clinical supervision however in that some managers will find that is difficult to maintain a handle on the individual clinical nurse specialist and clinical supervision process if supervision takes place outside the organisation.

Table 4.5: Advantages of external clinical supervision for clinical nurse specialists

The external validation of senior clinical practice is important

Objectivity is achieved by using an external clinical supervisory facilitator

Cross fertilisation of ideas-sharing of good practice, dissemination and innovative practices are assisted by collaboration not competition

Productive use of time to ensure clinical nurse specialists who may well be the fulcrum of clinical requirements and demands at this level

---

Clinical Nurse Specialist can be isolated as individuals. By the very nature of this role they are usually few in number and often are the most senior nurses in clinical practice. Clinical supervision may often require a combination of approaches in ways that might seem somewhat unorthodox for other nursing staff, they may use medical staff as part of their clinical supervision. Clinical nurse specialists who are likely to be the most senior clinically based nurses requiring clinical supervision, therefore have a restricted number of individuals who are able to provide them with clinical supervision. To meet clinical supervision requirements a different approach to the problem and a different solution is required. Think through your needs and who is the most appropriate person/s to provide clinical supervision, be resourceful and imaginative.

How could clinical supervision work for a sister/charge nurse on a children's ward?

The Clothier Report (1991) raised the issue of supervision for nurses working with sick children. The Department of Health (1992) also highlighted the need for professional supervision for staff working in child protection. Unlike social workers who have received supervision for many years, nurses have viewed supervision as something needed by those who are unable to cope (Byrne, 1995). In adult nursing, staff often need to work in pairs in order to carry out some of the physical care, very often children's nurses work alone and so direct supervision is difficult. Although many aspects of adult nursing call for difficult decisions to be taken and involve stressful and emotional events, it could be argued that in certain situations in children's nursing these decisions and events are far more traumatic because they involve the lives of children.

In addition to the traditional role of the nurse in the hospital ward a number of new roles for community paediatric nurses are developing. New roles which combine hospital and community care are also developing. Within the hospital setting specialist High Dependency and Intensive Care Units are relatively common place. Thus the breadth and intensity of children's nursing has developed almost beyond recognition of the role 15 years ago. Sensitive, skilled and formalised clinical supervision has become a crucially important issue for all paediatric nurses.

As a nurse in charge of a paediatric ward you will want to build upon existing supervisory systems or develop more formalised structures that ensure all staff in your area are receiving clinical supervision which is supportive, developmental and has a monitoring or quality control element within it.

Barton-Wright (1994) describes how, acting as a supervisor, could enable a charge nurse to maintain a clinical focus while devolving clinical autonomy to primary nurses. You and your team may prefer a cascading hierarchical structure of supervision whereby the H grade supervises the G, the G supervises the Fs and so on. This is fairly easy to implement as it follows existing structures, but you may feel that there are some disadvantages to this hierarchical approach. If you do not wish to use a hierarchical system of supervision and there is more than one children's ward or unit in your organisation you may wish to use staff in other areas to supervise. You could involve community staff e.g. health visitors and school nurses. Alternatively, you may wish to involve other professions, physiotherapists, play therapists or psychologists. You may choose someone from an entirely different speciality to act as your supervisor. These systems are more complex to implement in that they involve more than one ward and possibly other professions, but they do have certain advantages in the sort of relationships that are fostered.

Group supervision could work well in an area where people are working in isolation, it will help to build team work and encourage people to share ideas.

There is no right or wrong way to develop clinical supervision for children's nurses. The most important action is to involve your staff in its development, a bottom up approach, identify what it is you want clinical supervision to achieve and then plan a structure which best achieves those outcomes. Be realistic about issues such as time involvement, degree of choice, frequency and then proceed. Be prepared to run it for at least six months and then begin to evaluate it based on your identified outcomes. Then adapt your system based on your experience. The final point is that as the sister/charge nurse be careful that you do not over commit yourself. See your role as motivator, and facilitator. It may be tempting to act as supervisor to almost everyone, but do resist that. Involve all your staff from the beginning, maximise on their strengths, encourage and support them.

How could it work for a staff nurse on an intensive care unit?

The first thing to consider when developing a system of clinical supervision for staff nurses in an intensive care unit is that the needs of the staff nurses will vary depending upon their level of experience. There may be some staff nurses that are recently qualified or new to the intensive care setting. Other staff nurses may have post registration ITU qualifications and may have been working in the unit for many years, preferring the role of staff nurse to that of higher grades within the hierarchy. The focus and aims of clinical supervision will need to vary for each of these groups, if it does not and the same model and aims are imposed on all the staff nurses then it is unlikely to meet individuals specific needs. The next stage would be to identify the purpose of clinical supervision for each of the sub groups of the staff nurses. This could be done by getting the group to meet together and discuss what they wanted from clinical supervision. The question to ask is, what is the purpose of clinical supervision for this group of staff? Consider it under three headings, developmental needs, professional support, standard of practice. The purpose of clinical supervision in intensive care units includes:

- Developmental needs — for the inexperienced staff nurse the ITU is a frightening and complex world. Most ITU's have a development programme which identifies important and relevant skills that the inexperienced staff nurse needs to master. The development programme should identify the psychomotor skills, the underpinning knowledge and also the ethical / attitudinal issues of the ITU. The experienced staff nurses developmental needs will obviously go beyond these. These may vary according to individuals interest, some may want to focus on teaching, others on bereavement counselling or infection control, another may be interested in research, the list is almost endless

- Professional support — here the needs of the inexperienced and the experienced staff nurse will have a number of common areas, although they may also have individual support needs. The supervisee will need the opportunity to talk over clinical decisions that they have or are contemplating making. Working in an ITU setting combines two major sources of professional stress, firstly the stress of working with technology and critical situations and secondly is the intensity of the relationships that are demanded of the nurse by the relatives of the patients

- Standard of practice — the inexperienced staff nurse will want feedback on their clinical practice, this will often take the form of them working closely with a more experienced member of staff with direct observation of their work. This is not a managerial check up, but a formative developmental process which aims to help the less experienced person to develop and master the skills of ITU nursing. The experienced staff nurse will not necessarily need direct observation of their practice although this might be a part of their clinical supervision. For the more experienced staff nurse it is probably more useful to reflect upon their clinical practice discussing with a colleague the particular way they respond to certain situations.

Having identified the purpose of clinical supervision for the different groups it is then important to identify who is going to act as supervisor. It is important that the supervisee feels that they are able to influence who is going to be their supervisor. The key points in identifying supervisors is that they are people who want to take on the role, they have high standards of care and have greater experience than the supervisee.

The next stage to think through is that of the relationship and other ground rules that need to be defined between the supervisor and supervisee. The supervisee, supervisor and the unit manager need to be involved here. There will be certain ground rules that are common to all staff on the ITU unit and some of these may be common to all staff working within the hospital Trust.

The final stage to discuss is that of the time involvement and structure of how and when clinical supervision will happen. For the inexperienced staff nurse clinical supervision will probably need to be structured so that the supervisor is in fairly frequent contact with the supervisee. This may include working the same shifts for a certain proportion of the week with a specific meeting of an hour a week to reflect and concentrate on specific issues. For the more experienced staff nurse the scheduling of specific meetings does not need to be so frequent but they may need longer to discuss fully certain issues, so a meeting may be arranged for two hours every month.

Table 4.6: Implementing clinical supervision in an ITU

Are there different groups of staff nurses on the ITU? If so what are they?

What is the purpose of clinical supervision for each of these groups? Make sure that they are involved in these discussions and that something in not perscribed for them.

Who is going to act as supervisor for the different staff nurses?

What are the ground rules and the nature of the relationship between the supervisor and supervisee? Again remember to involve them in these decisions.

What is the time involvement and schedule for the implementation of supervision?

How could it work for a health visitor?

When thinking about how to implement supervision as a health visitor certain key principles should be thought through including:

- Everyone should be clear about the purpose or aims of supervision
- All those who will be involved should participate in the discussions about how to make supervision work
- The team characteristics should be considered - size; different grades and experience; specialist knowledge and skills etc.
- The pattern and nature of work should be explored — how it is organised; where the stresses are; new demands and skill requirements; type of client populations etc.

The last two points are about focusing on what it is that is special about the work that you do and how you are organised to do it. Certain themes are likely to emerge and these might include:

- Largely autonomous, independent practice — although health visitors work as part of a primary health care team and will work in partnership with other health visitors at times, most of their work may be carried out independently and in relative isolation from other practitioners

- Process rather than outcome-oriented practice — much of health visiting work is concerned with building helping relationships with clients with disparate needs. Outcomes are often highly client-specific, long-term and difficult to measure

- Absence of hierarchical team structure — although with any group of health visitors there is usually a range of experience there is little or no clearly defined hierarchy as in other nursing teams

- Multi-disciplinary elements — particularly in relation to child protection health visitors may, at times, work more closely with practitioners who are not nurses and who work within different organisations than with other health visitors or nurses. New developments in health visiting are beginning to see multi-disciplinary health visiting teams emerging in some areas. These may include RSCNs, Child Branch RNs, RGNs and nursery nurses.

Health visitors seeking to implement clinical supervision should consider these characteristics alongside the following: the functions or purpose of supervision.

An example of a model of supervision which focuses on the functions or purposes of supervision would be that developed by Proctor (undated) which identifies three interlocking functions of supervision:

- Formative - a learning process
- Restorative - supportive
- Normative - managerial or quality control.

The characteristics of the supervisory relationship for example Frankham's (1987),12–role model of supervisor functions.

Table 4.8: Frankham's (1987) 12–role model of supervisor fuctions

Monitor	Professional representation	Mentor
Manager	Teacher	Mirror
Evaluator	Analyst	Facilitator
Reviewer	Trainer	Therapist

The supervisory process

Models which have focused primarily on the process itself have been largely derived from counselling and psycho-therapy but may have much to offer nurses who work very closely with clients and families over fairly long periods of time as may often happen in health visiting, for example Hawkin and Shohet's (1989) two matrix model of supervision. This explores particular client interventions and nursing processes and also what occurs during the supervision process and how this can further enlighten understanding of nurse/client interactions.

Although these models are presented separately all these aspects of supervision need to be considered when making that final crucial decision about how supervision will be delivered. Only then are you in a position to consider the precise model of delivery which is likely to suit you best.

Table 4.8: Models of delivery of clinical supervision for health visitors

One–to–one with a more experienced health visitor acting as supervisor to a less experienced health visitor

One–to–one with a supervisor from a different discipline

One–to–one with two health visitors with similar levels of experience

Group supervision which may be:

- Peer groups within the team
- Peer groups across two or more teams
- Groups supervised by a more experienced supervisor eg. experienced health visitor, possibly a CPT supervising a group of less experienced health visitors
- Team supervision involving the whole health visiting team
- Team supervision involving all or part of the multi-disciplinary team

Network supervision which provides occasional external input into any of the above for example accessing health visitors from different team to explore particular areas of practice or using specialists to provide supervision for areas of specialist practice eg. child protection.

Table 4.9 highlights examples of what might work with different groups:

Table 4.9

Type of group	Type of supervision
Small groups of similarly experienced health visitors	One–to–one peer supervision or peer group supervision
Large group of health visitors with different levels of experience	Two or more peer groups with a more experienced practitioner giving supervision to a number of less experienced health visitors
Multi-disciplinary health visiting team	Team supervision within the team

Other issues that may help your thinking include:

- Time and other practical constraints — group supervision involves significantly less time out across the whole team. Particularly where there are relatively few potential supervisors this may be a much more realistic option than one–to–one supervision. Availability of rooms and fixed commitments like clinics need to be considered when deciding who should supervise whom and where. Health visitors often have relatively infrequent scheduled contact times but do tend to have planned commitments. Careful planning of these can provide windows of opportunity for supervision, but it does have to be made an absolute priority

- Involvement with clients and families with complex needs — the opportunity to reflect in-depth on the health visiting interventions, processes and inter-relationships with these clients and to explore alternative approaches is crucial to providing appropriate care and reducing risk in vulnerable families. It may be useful to supplement a model of peer group supervision with some one–to–one sessions and/or to access supervision from other related professions eg. social work or a specialist nurse eg. psychiatric nurse

- Different disciplines within the health visiting team — although team supervision may be the main model adopted within a multi-disciplinary team it is essential to promote access to other experienced practitioners from the same discipline. This may be achieved by arranging peer group supervision for example for a number of nursery nurses across several teams and/or by accessing supervision from an external source

- Developing public health role and specialist health visitors — some health visitors may be developing their roles in relation to community health. It may be useful to supplement peer supervision with one–to–one supervision with a health visitor from elsewhere who has greater experience in this field or with other local experts. Similarly, other health visitors who have adopted specialist roles eg. working with travelling families or the homeless, may find it helpful to establish group or one–to–one supervision with other specialist health visitors working in a similar area of practice across a number of Trusts , or to develop multi-disciplinary supervision with other non-health visiting practitioners in the field.

Clinical supervision can be adapted in many different ways to meet your specific needs. Identify what your needs are and what you want from clinical supervision. Think through the various ways in which a system of clinical supervision could be practically implemented within your team and then make clinical supervision work for you.

How could it work for a practice nurse?

Clinical supervision is particularly relevant to practice nurses and will directly address some of the difficulties currently experienced by the unique nature of their employment situation (Cook, 1996). Frequently working in relative professional isolation often leads to a lack of support in addressing the issues of development, responsibility for practice and safety of care defined in *A Vision for the Future* (DoH, 1993). Clinical supervision can provide that vital support mechanism for nurses in the demanding environment of a busy general practice and offer a forum for discussion of clinical and quality issues.

The lack of hierarchical structure offers an ideal opportunity for clinical supervision to be undertaken in a supportive rather than managerial or academic way and used effectively it should enable practice nurses to continue to work as independent practitioners with the benefit of the knowledge that they are competent in their role. It can also be directly utilised as a tool to develop the reflective practice now required to maintain registration by demonstration in a professional profile.

Another issue specific to practice nurses is their direct employment by a general practitioner who has historically often become mentor as well as manager. This complex relationship may make it difficult for the individual nurse to suggest another system for supervision, but it is important not to let this become a barrier. General practitioners also have quality of care at the forefront of their role and any system which can maintain and improve the care of the practice population by safeguarding standards and improving efficiency and effectiveness should be met with positive encouragement. Discussion with general practitioner employers can be aided by the use of resources and research such as this book or the folder *Clinical Supervision — A Resource Pack* (NHS Executive, March, 1996).

When considering how to undertake clinical supervision each practice nurse should look at their particular employment and professional circumstances. The range of options available enables flexibility to choose that which best suits each individual situation. Five main systems of clinical supervision have been identified by Houston (1990).

1. One–to–one session with a peer

2. One–to–one sessions with an expert supervisor from the same discipline

3. One–to–one sessions with an expert supervisor from a different discipline

4. Group supervision with or without a trained/external supervisor

5. Network supervision between individuals or groups who do not work together on a daily basis

One–to–one peer

This system can be very convenient particularly when more than one nurse is employed in a practice enabling them to supervise each other. Two isolated nurses at neighbouring practices could also join up in this way. However UKCC (1996) guidelines indicate that preparation of supervisors is crucial to the success of clinical supervision and the King's Fund states that:

All supervisors should be given opportunities to receive training and learn the skills that are needed to provide supervision that is both constructive and supportive.

(Kohner,1995)

Therefore the peer support system is not ideal as neither of the nurses would necessarily have received any training. If implemented as an initial model while waiting for training to become available care should be taken to avoid the development of a narrow vision and input which only enhances professional isolation or damaging working relationships through lack of supervision skills.

One–to–one same discipline

This would be the preferred system for many practice nurses being regarded as a less threatening and safer environment than the group as well as having a supervisor that fully understands the role. The feasibility of this system depends on the local commitment to training sufficient practice nurse supervisors followed by enabling the time and resources required for them to undertake the work. In some areas the supervisors could be linked to training practices or become a natural extension of existing practice nurse trainers, mentors or practice teachers. Availability by area could also be considered utilising localities or commissioning groups of general practitioners.

One–to–one different disciplines

Despite concern about overlapping the roles of employer and supervisor this system could involve the general practitioner, possibly a partner not undertaking a direct managerial function for the practice nurse. Alternatively this system enables the practice nurse to explore the arrangements made by local Trusts and depending on their structures and agreements seek to obtain supervision from another community nurse colleague such as the district nurse, health visitor, school or psychiatric nurse. This route may also lead to the benefits of strengthened links and clearer understanding of role between the primary healthcare nursing team.

Group supervision

Group supervision enables issues and experiences to be shared which can be powerfully supportive if the supervisor has group facilitation skills as well as those related to supervision itself. The issues surrounding time commitment and number of supervisors required are largely surmounted as long as the difficulties of arranging a group meeting and having a large number (recommended 6–8) of nurses out of the clinical area at the same time can be overcome. Many practices now have a meeting room which could be used as a regular venue for a large single practice group or a system of rotation set up for group meetings of nurses from different practices. This system also allows for sharing resources such as journals and can be structured to meet group training and development needs as well as offering support to individuals.

Network supervision

Network supervision can be linked to one of the other systems and examples can be seen in both one–to–one peer and group sections. The formation of networks enables ready access to clinical supervision for practice nurses encouraging links across traditional role boundaries as well as the workplace locality. Where a practice nurse has particular skills and expertise additional supervision from a different area of practice may be beneficial. A matrix of networking enables an appropriate supervisor to be identified and accessed as required.

Having decided on the structure of the clinical supervision the next step is to consider the content or focus of the sessions. *Table 4.10* examines possible areas for discussion.

Table 4.10: Areas for discussion in practice nurse supervision

Clinical	Immunisation protocols,cervical cytology audit, recognising depression, new asthma guidelines
Professional	Confidentiality, portfolio development, expanding role and accountability, boundaries with medical staff
Organisational	Workload issues, profiling skills, reviewing job descriptions, developing teams and team leaders

Clinical supervision for practice nurses - getting started

The following summarises practical tips that may also help practice nurses to get started when looking at how to incorporate clinical supervision into their practice.

- Talk to general practitioner employers about the advantages of clinical supervision utilising resources and research

- Contact the local nurse advisor to find out about any new initiatives and developments in the area

- Find out how arrangements are made for clinical supervision with other members of the primary health care team eg. district nurse or community psychiatric nurse

- Discuss clinical supervision with other practice nurses utilising existing local groups and meetings

- Remember clinical supervision can be flexible to meet the needs of each individual practice nurse by a 'mix and match' of models

- Do not forget to consider how evaluation could be carried by measuring efficiency, standards, job satisfaction or understanding of role.

How could it work for someone working in a nursing home?

By now you will have accepted that there is no one model of clinical supervision that is appropriate to all areas of nursing. Equally, there is no one template for a nursing home. The range, from small single independent homes, to corporate organisations, with a network of homes across the country, produces complexity of management structures, philosophies and financial status as diverse as each home. Proportionate to this will be the owners/managers understanding of, and commitment to, clinical supervision and its development.

In its publication *Nursing Homes: Nursing Values* (RCN, 1996) the RCN did much to dispel the perception that nurses working with older adults are less skilled than their colleagues in the acute specialties. It clearly identified the vast range of roles that the trained nurse must fulfill within the nursing home setting, and highlighted the complex range of services that must be available and adaptable in ensuring that the residents' needs are met. In March 1995, there were 42,400 whole time equivalent registered and enrolled nurses employed in nursing homes in England (Laing, 1996), and experience shows that, for a multiplicity of reasons, this is increasing. This confirms Nazarko's (1994) view that nursing homes are the nurse led units of the future, both numerically and in terms of their potential, and therefore the responsibility for their development in terms of competencies, professional development, accountability and support for our colleagues rests with each of us.

Negotiation with owners/managers will need to be undertaken with regard to training, time and the financial commitment that this entails. Larger homes may already have training arrangements that can be tapped into, but smaller homes may find the concept daunting. This need not, however, be a stumbling block nor should it be seen as a justification for lack of action. Discussion must take place among the nurses to identify which model is appropriate or, indeed, obtainable. The number of nurses employed varies with the size of the establishment, which may have a direct bearing on which model is implemented. It may be possible to network with other homes, but the present culture may make that difficult.

Under the UKCC's Post Registration Education and Practice (PREP) Regulations (1995), nurses are required to be proactive in ensuring their own on–going professional development, part of which must be a continuous assessment of personal levels of functioning. Sometimes it can be difficult to evaluate our own level of function realistically. We are all subject to pressure at work, family commitments and our own fluctuating health status. Sometimes we work in isolation, and these situations can be compounded by the mistaken, but still commonly held, theory that the nurse who indicates the need for support, is simply not managing. Clinical supervision gives us a genuine chance to despatch this myth, along with the defensive practice that it engenders. It offers us the opportunity to place a value upon ourselves, and in so doing, enhance our value of both colleagues and residents.

In the large corporate nursing homes, it may be possible to obtain clinical supervision in its truest form because of the number of nurses involved and the training support available. In many homes, where the nurses are few and bed occupancy controls the money available, or the owner/manager's perception of the value of clinical supervision, nurses may well need to remind them of the part that skilled nursing plays in the provision of continuing care and ultimately, in the reputation of their home.

It may be that, initially, nurses may have to demonstrate their own commitment to enhancing their practice and this can be done in a number of ways.

Reflective practice

Which is similar to critical incident analysis. This can, however, expose incompetence and vulnerability, so needs to be controlled and understood. The work of Johns (1995) would be of assistance for those wishing to work alone.

Peer Group Support

This can be done by two nurses of the same experience meeting together for a one–to–one relationship where the roles are reversed alternately. Or by three or more nurses meeting to jointly reflect on their work and achievements. As this does not involve a trained supervisor, the following must be understood and observed:

- The meetings must be on a regular basis
- There must be an agreed agenda to reflect on their practice
- Care must be taken to remain objective and to take responsibility for identifying areas that need attention.

Peer evaluation can be an extremely effective tool for promoting good practice, but only if it is structured to allow objective and constructive feedback. If it is to be productive, it will require commitment and trust, and an understanding that it is the practice and not the person that is being reviewed. It will require, courage to give and receive constructive criticism, and the ability to balance this with accolades. Insight is required if we are to avoid the imposition of our standards on to colleagues and to accept that cultural , religious and sexual differences will shape our values and norms.

Although peer supervision can be seen to be the least expensive method of securing clinical supervision, consideration must be given to its major disadvantage. Participants need to accept that, unless great care is exercised it will allow the perpetuation of poor practices which other models would explore more rigorously.

You care for some of society's most vulnerable citizens and your role is expanding constantly, without the support and development that comes with clinical supervision, it will become increasingly difficult to be sure that your practice is safe and that you are, indeed, the residents advocate.

5

Evaluating the benefits of clinical supervision

Jim Dooher, John Fowler, Ann-Marie Phillips and Alison Wells

How does clinical supervision benefit the supervisee?

The benefits of clinical supervision for the supervisee may not be immediately clear for those people who feel time away from the patient is time wasted. The opportunity to stand back and take stock of our professional lives while being paid for it, was almost unheard of until the introduction of clinical supervision.

Clinical supervision is a gift of time from your organisation. There is no obligation for them to provide this opportunity, apart from a desire to see improvements in your personal and professional development and ultimately the quality of patient care you provide.

Good quality nursing cannot be sustained by its delivery alone, it needs to be planned and given consideration, no matter how routine the task or familiar the process. Clinical supervision offers the opportunity for your working practice to be constantly updated through regular meetings which share group or individual expertise, and benefit from the real experience which underpins it. This should be considered a golden opportunity for supervisees to learn the experience of others, without incurring the risk of making the same mistakes. Darley (1995) suggested that clinical supervision could provide the constructive means to assist with a practice deficit and to change that practice thereby avoiding the need to take the matter further. This endorsement of addressing clinical shortfalls outside of managerial control, may not sit comfortably with some managers, however this factor may improve feelings of safety for both supervisor and supervisee and in turn, develops the confidence to expose weaknesses, share worries and resolve issues without the fear of managerial intervention. The nature of what themes may be discussed will be identified in the supervision contract, a document which not only sets the parameters and defines the nature of the relationship, but protects the supervisee from any abuse of the process.

Feeling comfortable with clinical supervision may take a little time to achieve, and experience has shown that sharing ideas, opinions, attitudes or feelings about working practice, may highlight tensions between individuals and within the team. Clinical supervision provides a forum to discuss these tensions, and at the same time an opportunity to resolve them.

There are many additional benefits for the supervisee, some of which were highlighted by Farrington (1995) in that, practitioners can be enabled to develop clinical competencies and standards through clinical supervision, that staff are better supported, which results in reduced stress and less burnout.

A study by Berg *et al* (1994) demonstrated that systematic clinical supervision and individually planned care, encouraged nurses to reflect both emotionally and cognitively on their provision of nursing care; it stimulated creativity and decreased negative outcomes like tedium and burnout.

Resolving work stress, within the workplace, is arguably a key tool in our professional survival kit, and if accompanied by a feeling of positive self value supported through regular sessions, this may influence job satisfaction and in turn, the frequency of job changes, enabling the supervisee to devote time to patient care rather than looking for another job. It was recognised by Revicki and May (1989) that work related social support is of some significance in decreasing the impact of stress and job strain.

Clinical supervision provided on an individual, triadic or group basis aims to assist the supervisee to do their job better, provide better informed care, born from both theory and practical experience, enhancing our interactions with patients and colleagues to improve clinical outcomes.

Table 5.1: Key points

- Professional support

- Role development

- Improved confidence to define and set clinical standards

- Intra– and inter–professional networking

- Permission to be innovative with the ways you organise your working day and the interventions you provide

- Improved job control and satisfaction

- The opportunity to exchange professional issues and ideas

- Developing a sharing culture with colleagues.

How does clinical supervision benefit the supervisor?

The process of supervision can be time–consuming, but the author's own experience of supporting people in their careers has been very rewarding. It is also very flattering when staff approach you to become their supervisor. The process of clinical supervision means that I have to listen closely to what the supervisee is saying, something I'm not usually very good at, I have felt my confidence develop and I've generally enjoyed the experience.

The supervisor can benefit in these and a number of other ways. There is a great deal of satisfaction to be gained from helping someone to develop clinically or professionally. Taking on the role of the supervisor means you have to keep yourself up to date and examine your own practice. The process will be challenging and will help you to think clearly about your practice and develop new skills. As a supervisor you could become recognised as an 'expert' and could have some influence over the profession, even if only in a small way (Inskipp and Proctor, 1995). Supervision helps build teamwork and improves your relationship with other members of staff. Supporting someone need not be a one way process, it can lead to mutual support and benefit.

As a supervisor, you will also have to choose a supervisor for yourself so you will also benefit from being a supervisee.

> *To be asked to be a clinical supervisor, I felt was an honour but a great responsibility. As a clinical nurse specialist, I feel I have to offer knowledge and experience of how to 'grow' professionally. When these skills are passed on and the supervisee begins to incorporate them into their own clinical experience, then the sense of achievement is shared.*

Clinical supervision is a two way process. Ideas on how to develop personally and professionally can be used for the supervisor as well as the supervisee.

Ann Spanswick

Asthma Nurse Specialist – Leicester

How does clinical supervision benefit the clinical area?

The link between clinical supervision and patient outcomes is important if nurses are to justify the supervision process to managers. The need to evaluate supervision therefore remains a priority. Trust Nurses Executives (Butterworth and Bishop, 1994) have suggested looking at the impact of supervision through some existing mechanisms, such as; sickness rates, complaints, and staff and patient satisfaction. However the evaluation of this process is still in its infancy and the multi-site clinical supervision evaluation project demonstrates the complexity of trying to research clinical supervision (Butterworth *et al*, 1997). Research illustrating the benefits of supervision however remains important in an environment where nurses wish to use evidence based practice to justify their actions.

Both a quantitative and a qualitative approach is required to evaluate the supervision process, (Butterworth, 1996). Statistics such as sickness rates and complaints, are important to examine, although causation between supervision and reduced sickness rates may be difficult to prove because of a multitude of variables. Looking at a range of quantitative measures before and after the introduction of supervision, while trying to reduce variables such as nursing establishments, patient through put, or the introduction of new working practices is difficult. Research into clinical supervision has a 'chicken and egg' quality. Trusts are worried about introducing such a system, because of cost and the lack of quantitative data, and yet the real benefits of supervision are unlikely to be realised until the process is incorporated into the working practices of all nurses. It needs to be realised that the benefits to the profession are likely to be long term.

On a medical ward the author monitored sickness and complaints a year before and a year after the implementation of supervision and there was no significant difference between the two. This information needs to be collected over a longer period of time, but it is unlikely that quantitative data on its own will truly reflect the benefits of the supervision process.

Where a qualitative approach is taken, the benefits to individual nurses working in clinical areas are more apparent. One nurse who was finding work very demanding and difficult, while also trying to study for an academic course, said that on one occasion if it had not been for the support and help that she was receiving in her supervision she 'would have gone off sick'. Therefore while the author's sickness rate did not appear to alter when supervision was implemented, if it had not been for the supervision process, the rate may have actually increased.

At the end of a ten month period of supervision many of the supervisees who where practising in the author's area of work, actually reflected upon some of their thoughts, feelings and experiences of the supervision process. The following are some extracts:

> I have been qualified for nine years and during this time I have gradually distanced myself from patients that I have cared for. I did this consciously to protect myself from the stress and emotional pain felt. Over the last year this has changed.......through the support,

encouragement and challenges given by clinical supervision, I am able to analyse my nursing actions and learn from them. I have identified my educational needs and it (clinical supervision) has given me confidence in myself. I do not hide behind my uniform as though it were a suit of armour, but let me, the person shine through.

When I actually started the clinical supervision sessions and learnt more about the theory I actually saw the benefits that could come from the sessions.......At a time when I felt particularly despondent about some nursing issues.....during the hour's session with my supervisor I was reassured that it was perfectly natural that I felt like that, which was very supportive and beneficial to me.

There were noticeable changes in the performance of qualified nurses who were undergoing clinical supervision. On the whole they appeared to became more confident about their abilities and practices. Decision making skills increased with their confidence and they questioned and became more critical of the care they delivered. Handy (1994) states:

..if we want to reconcile our humanity with our economics, we have to find a way to what is personal and local, so that we have a chance to make a difference, that we matter along with those around us.

Clinical supervision gives nurses this opportunity. Research into the effects of supervision on patient outcomes and the nursing workforce needs to continue. One way to relate supervision to patient outcomes, is to ask nurses in supervision to fill in a form/questionnaire every time they can directly relate their supervision to a change in practice and patient outcome.

The real benefit of clinical supervision is that it allows nurses real time to reflect and examine their practices, as without doubt, nurses in the course of their daily work do expose themselves to situations and relationships that are demanding and stressful (Rowan, 1987). As one supervisee reflects:

It has been a very comforting feeling to know that someone in this large organisation is interested in me, the person, as well as me the professional. I believe that every person involved in providing health care would benefit from clinical supervision.

How does clinical supervision benefit the hospital/Trust?

The NHS Management Executive published, *A Vision for the Future* (Department of Health, 1993). It acknowledged in section 3.22 that,

New ways must be found to support nurses, midwives and health visitors in maintaining and developing high standards of practice as they increasingly work in different ways and in different environments.

Having identified this as a very real need and something that cannot be ignored, the document goes on to suggest that clinical supervision is a way of providing support in the development of clinical practice:

Clinical supervision is a term used to describe a formal process of professional support and learning which enables individual practitioners to develop knowledge and competence, assume responsibility for their own practice and enhance consumer

protection and the safety of care in complex clinical situations. (section 3.27)

Try to view the situation from the perspective of the chief executive of your hospital or Trust. Visualise the entire workforce that are involved in direct patient care (possibly all the others as well) working within a system whereby each person has regular clinical supervision which offers professional support, development and monitoring of standards. If I were the chief executive then this would give me the knowledge and security of a workforce in which all were supported, developed and monitored in a positive and developmental way. This is truly a positive vision. If a hospital or Trust had such a system up and running then this is a objective and tangible way of demonstrating to the public 'enhanced consumer protection and the safety of care in complex clinical situations'.

The UKCC (1996) also acknowledges that the benefits of clinical supervision are not limited to patients, clients or practitioners. They suggest that if implemented it, *'should contribute effectively to organisational objectives'* and should make a significant contribution to *'clinical risk management'*. Though it is important to note that neither the NHS Executive, nor the UKCC are promoting clinical supervision as a management system whose prime purpose is to achieve some management objective. The prime purpose of clinical supervision is to enable practitioners to develop professional practice within an increasingly complex environment.

Dr David Clutterbuck (1995) of the European Mentoring Centre discusses the rapid expansion of such systems in the business world and identifies benefits not only for the mentees and mentors but also for the organisation. The organisation gains 'because people in new jobs become more effective, more quickly. They also stay longer, employee turnover falls when people are helped to fit in and when people feel supported'. He suggests that a climate where finding ways to help people grow becomes instinctive for managers at all levels.

Table 5.2: Key points

- Enhances consumer protection and the safety of care

- Contribution to organisational objectives

- People in new jobs become more effective, more quickly

- Potential reduction of staff turnover

- Encourages a positive working climate.

The health care profession relies significantly on people to deliver its service. If clinical supervision were to help people feel more positive about their work and help them develop a positive developmental culture, or reduce staff turnover by only 5% then the implications for the Trust would be significant. However these hospital/Trust benefits are only likely to occur if clinical supervision is in place for all staff and implemented in a way that makes it a positive and meaningful experience for the supervisee. If clinical supervision was implemented or practised in an inappropriate way it could easily become a paper exercise and therefore a waste of everyone's time.

How does clinical supervision benefit patients/clients?

Professor Butterworth who is co-ordinating a national evaluative study on clinical supervision (Butterworth *et al*, 1997) acknowledges the ideal research will be that in which clinical supervision is shown to have an impact on patient outcome (Butterworth, 1996). He goes on to state however that the complexity of the environment that surrounds clinical supervision and the fact that in most areas it is in a very early stage of development, makes any attempt to measure its effects upon patients fraught with difficulty.

The ideal way to evaluate clinical supervision and so answer the question of whether it has any benefits for patients would be to set up a randomised controlled trial. There would be two wards, identical in every way. Over a period of a year they would admit exactly the same number of patients. For every, 'patient A' that was admitted to one ward, 'patient A1' would be admitted to the other ward. Patient A and A1 would have to be matched so that they were the same age, had the same beliefs, attitudes, qualifications, jobs, social life, families etc. This would have to be true for all patients admitted. Each patient would need to be matched exactly with a patient admitted onto the other ward. Then all the staff would need to be matched in the same way, not only nurses but all other staff as well. Having established two identical wards one would be deemed the control ward the other the experimental. Clinical supervision would be implemented in the experimental ward but not in the other. The experimental ward should not know that it is the experimental ward because that may influence the results. Nor should the staff or patients from the two wards mix. Next some way of reliably measuring the effects of the 'independent variable' (clinical supervision) on patients would need to be developed. This could be patient satisfaction surveys, recovery rates, infection rates, stress levels etc. Only then would a methodological purist researcher begin to be in a position to make a statement regarding the implications of clinical supervision for patient care. This would then have to be repeated for community settings, learning disabilities and any other areas which were a little different from the original experiment.

This scenario is obviously an extreme perspective, the opposite view would be to say, 'I just know patients will benefit/or not benefit from clinical supervision, I just feel it'. Somewhere in-between these two extremes is the mixing of clinical experience and evaluative evidence to give an informed professional judgement. Even so we can only really speculate as to what the benefits to patient care are. It is probably easier to see the effects upon patients if all the elements being promoted within clinical supervision were removed from the current system. Imagine the effects on patient care if all professional support was removed, all on–going development, all monitoring of standards. Patient care would soon deteriorate beyond all recognition.

Platt-Koch (1986) writing about clinical supervision for psychiatric nurses states that,

> *It is a disservice to both the patient and the nurse to attempt to do psychiatric treatment without adequate clinical supervision.*

Is this not true for all patients and clients and not just those with a mental health problem?

However clinical supervision is not some panacea that will allow staff to deliver high quality care with inappropriate resources. Professor Bishop, a nursing officer in the nursing directorate of the NHS Executive states that,

> *While clinical supervision will help nurses to achieve the best level of care possible, it cannot compensate for inadequate facilities, for poor management or for unmotivated staff. However it will create a culture within which nurses can flourish, if they are willing to embrace it, and if management is supportive.*

> (Bishop, 1994).

It seems probable that a well structured, supportive clinical supervision system which addresses the needs of all staff involved in the delivery of health care will have an indirect positive effect on patient care. As we begin to develop and refine clinical supervision we need to have on–going evaluations which focus on the process and outcomes for both staff and patients.

Appendix I - a sample contract for clinical supervision

There are many good reasons for having a contract for your clinical supervision these include:

- It is important to legitimise and formalise you clinical supervisory relationship

- It provides a secure framework from the start from which you can move forward

- It creates a structure which you can work with and expand upon

- It allows for changes without personalising issues

- It demonstrates commitment from both parties and management

- It allows you to structure goals and monitor your development of knowledge and skills.

As a guide you should include some or all of the following information in the contract with your supervisor/ supervisee:

- How often you are going to meet

- Approximately how long will each session be

- The date you agreed the contract

- How long the contract will run for before you review it (If you have just started you might want to review it often or even each time you meet)

- Where you will usually meet

- Ground rules (negotiated by either party) often at the beginning of clinical supervisory relationships

there are many ground rules as each party is a little
unsure of what to expect

- Any notes, for example as a guide to the content of
your sessions.

There follows an example of a contract which you are free
to copy or amend. If you have access to a word processor it
can be fun to create your own version. If you photocopy
the example it is best to copy the two pages back to back
so that you only have one piece of paper.

Supervision Contract

Supervisor:

Supervisee:

Frequency of session (nominal):

Nominal length of session:

Usual venue:

Date of contract:

Date of next contract review:

Notes:

Supervisor signature: _____

Supervisee signature: _____

Rules of this contract

Compliance

In the event of non-compliance with this supervision contract the following procedures will apply:

1. An informal reminder will be given by either party and a further date arranged

2. If the above does not result in resolution, a written reminder from either party will be issued

3. If this fails to resolve the difficulty, as a last resort:
   a. The supervisee will write to his/her line manager requesting that supervision be arranged

   OR

   b. The supervisor will write to the supervisee's line manager requesting intervention.

Appendix II - evaluation of clinical supervision

This evaluation form is designed to help you and your supervisor reflect upon the proccess of clinical supervision. The supervisee and supervisor should each fill in the form and then meet together to discuss their responses. The supervisor should fill in the form from the perspective of the supervisee – that is, how do they feel the supervisee will respond to each question.

If you wish to use the evaluation form to collect feedback from a larger group of people then the form could be completed anonymously and responses collated seperately for supervisors and supervisees.

Evaluation of clinical supervision between

Name   and   **Name**

Aim of clinical supervision

To provide time for the supervisee to look at and reflect upon, what happens at work, and external events which effect work, in order to maximise supervisee's effectiveness in providing a service to his/her client group.

   1. Overall was this aim achieved?

      Not at all   [ ]   Not as expected   [ ]

      As expected [ ]   Better than expected [ ]

Content (tick as appropriate)

To what extent did clinical supervision have an affect upon the following areas of your life:

		Some	None
2	Personnal development	[ ]	[ ]
3	Professional development	[ ]	[ ]
4	Clinical management issues	[ ]	[ ]
5	Organisational management issues	[ ]	[ ]
6	Clinical issues relating to specific patients	[ ]	[ ]
7	General clinical issues	[ ]	[ ]
8	Personnal issues	[ ]	[ ]

General ground rules

9. How often did you initially agree to meet?

10. To what extent was this fulfilled?
    As arranged [ ]   More often [ ]   Less often [ ]

11. How long was the average length of your clinical supervision sessions?

12. Was this:
    Longer [ ]   Shorter [ ] Same [ ]
    as initially discussed.

13. Did you feel that confidentiality was maintained?
    Yes [ ]   No [ ]

14. Were any of the sessions cancelled?
    Most of them [ ]   Some of them [ ]
    None of them [ ]

Supervision styles

15. What sort of style or form did supervision take
    (please tick as many as appropriate)

Giving advice   [ ]   Giving information   [ ]

Teaching   [ ]   Supportive   [ ]

Challenging   [ ]   Reflective   [ ]

Providing a different perspective   [ ]

Allowing me to talk about areas of concern   [ ]

Encouraged me to think about areas I had not thought   [ ]
about before

16. To what extent did the supervisor intervene:
    Too much [ ]   Enough [ ]   Too little [ ]

17. Supervision was:
    Too directive   [ ]   Just right [ ]
    Not directive enough [ ]

Influence of clinical supervision on practice

18. Do you feel that your experience of clinical
    supervision has influenced your clinical practice?
    Not at all   [ ]   To some extent   [ ]
    To a large extent [ ]

Can you give an example of how clinical supervision has influenced your clinical practice?

References

Allitt Inquiry (1991) *Independent inquiry relating to deaths and injuries on children's ward at Grantham and Kesteven Hospital during the period February to April 1991.* HMSO. London

Atkin K, Lunt N (1993) A census of direction. *Nurs Times* **89**(42): 38–41

Atkin K, Lunt N (1995) Training and education in practice nursing. *Nurs Educ Today* **15**(6):406–13

Atkins S, Murphy K (1993) Reflection: a review of the literature. *J Adv Nurs* **18**:1188–92

Atkins S, Williams A (1995) Registered Nurses' experiences of mentoring undergraduate nursing students. *J Adv Nurs* **21** 1006–15

Barber P, Norman I (1987) Skills in supervision. *Nurs Times* Jan 14 56–7

Barton-Wright (1994) Clinical supervision in primary nursing. *Br J Nurs* **3:**123–30

Berg A, Welander Hansun U, Halberg IR (1994) Nurses' creativity, tedium and burnout during one year of clinical supervision and implementation of individually planned nursing care. *J Adv Nurs* 20:742–9

Bishop V (1994) Clinical supervision for an accountable profession. *Nurs Times* **90**(39):35–7

British Association for Counselling (1988) *Code of Ethics and Practice for the Supervision of Counsellors.* BAC, Rugby

British Association for Counselling (1994) Information Leaflet

Butcher K (1995) Taking notes. *Nurs Times* **91**(26): 33

Butterworth T, Faugier J (1992) *Clinical Supervision and Mentorship in Nursing.* Chapman and Hall, London

Butterworth T (1994) Preparing to take on clinical supervision. *Nurs Standard* **8**(5): 232–4

Butterworth T (1995) *Clinical supervision in nursing, midwifery and health visiting: development contracts and monitoring: a second briefing paper*

Butterworth T (1996) Primary attempts at research - based evaluation of clinical supervision. *NT Research* 1(2: 96–101

Butterworth T, Bishop V (ed) (1994) *Clinical Supervision : A report of the Trust Nurse Executives' Workshops.* NHS Executive, London

Butterworth T, Carson J, White E, *et al* (1997) *It Is Good To Talk . An Evaluation Study in England and Scotland.* The University of Manchester

Byrne C (1995) A model for supervision. *Primary Health Care* 5(1): 21–2

Carthy J (1994) Bandwagons roll. *Nurs Standard* 8(3): 48–9

Clark AD, Simpson RG (1997) *The role of health care assistants in community mental health teams, (the support of elderly clients at home).* LMHS unpublished document.

Clarkson P, Gilbert M (1991) The training of counsellor trainers and supervisors. In Dryden W, Thorne B (eds) *Training and Supervision for Counselling in Action.* Sage Publications, London.

Clutterbuck D (1995) *Consenting Adults - Making the most of Mentoring.* Broadcasting Support Services, Channel 4, London

Cook R (1996) Series on clinical supervision. *Prac Nurs* 7(15 and 16): 12–4

Cowling L, Evans J (1995) Bench marks. *Nurs Times* 91(26): 31–2

Darley M (1995) Clinical supervision *Nurs Man* 2(3): 14–6

Darling L (1984) What do nurses want in a mentor? *J Nurs Admin* 14(10): 42–4

Davies P (1993) Value yourself — regular clinical supervision can help reduce stress. *Nurs Times* 89(4) 52

Deming W E (1982) *Quality, Productivity and Competitive Position.* MTI Centre for Advance Engineering Studies

Department of Health (1992) *Guidance for Senior Nurses, Health Visitors and Midwives* HMSO,London

Department of Health (1993) *A Vision for the Future. The Nursing, Midwifery and Health Visiting Contribution to Health Care.* HMSO, London

Department of Health (1994) CNO letter 94(5) *Clinical supervision for the nursing and health visiting professions.* HMSO, London

Department of Health (1995) *Clinical Supervision* (Conference Proceedings from a national conference, Birmingham) NHS Executive, London

Dewar BJ, Clark JM (1992) The role of the paid non-professional nursing helper: a review of the literature. J Adv Nurs **17:** 113–20

Dewer B (1992) Skill muddle?...Skill mix?....Roles of trained and untrained staff. *Nurs Times* **88**(33): 24–7

Dryden W (1991) *Dryden on Counselling - Training & Supervision* Whurr Publishers, London & New Jersey

Earnshaw G (1995) Mentorship: the students' views. *Nurs Educ Today* **15:** 274–9

Ekstein R, Wallenstein R (1972) *The Teaching and Learning of Psychotherapy.* International Universities Press, New York

Evans D (1981) Supervisory Management. Holt Business Texts

Farrington A (1995) Defining and setting the parameters of clinical supervision. *Br J Nurs* **4**(15): 875

Faugier J (1992) The supervisory relationship. In Butterworth CA, Fauiger J (eds) *Clinical Supervision and Mentorship in Nursing.* Chapman & Hall

Faugier J, Butterworth (1994) *Clinical Supervision: A Position Paper.* The University of Manchester

Fisher M (1996) Using reflective practice in clinical supervision. *Prof Nurs* **11**(7): 443–4

Fowler J (1995) Nurses' perceptions of the elements of good supervision. *Nurs Times* **91**(22): 33–7

Fowler J (1996) The organisation of clinical supervision within the nursing profession. *J Adv Nurs* **23:** 471–8

Fowler J (1996a) How to use models of clinical supervision in practice. *Nurs Standard* **10**(29): 42–7

Fowler J (1996b) Clinical supervision: What do you do after you say hello? *Br J Nurs* **5**(6): 382–5

Fox P (1995) Nursing developments: Trust nurses' views. *Nurs Standard* **9**(18): 30–4

Frankham H (1987) *Aspects of Supervision, Counsellor, Satisfaction, Utility and Defensiveness and Tasks in Supervision.* Dissertation, Roehampton Institute, University of Surrey

Gadell C (1986) Clinical supervision for psychiatric nurses. *Ohio Nurs Rev* **61**(9): 13

Handy C (1994) *The Empty Raincoat.* Hutchinson

Hawkins P, Shoet R (1989) *Supervision in the Helping Professions.* Open University Press, Milton Keynes

Hawkins P, Shohet R (1991) Approaches to the supervision of counsellors: The supervisory relationship. In Dryden W, Throne, B *Training and Supervision for Counselling in Action*

Heron J, (1990) *Helping the Client. A Creative Practical Guide.* SAGE Publications, London.

Hill J, (1989) Supervision in the Caring Professions; a literature review. *Com Psych Nurs J* **9**(5): 9-15

Houston G (1990) *Supervision and Counselling* The Rochester Foundation, London

Inskipp F, Proctor B (1995) *Becoming a Supervisor.* 36–41 Cascade

Ivey A (1977) Foreword in *Supervision of Applied Training Comparative Review.* Kurpius DJ, *et al* Greenwood Press, London

Johns C (1993) Professional supervision. *J Nurs Man* **1**: 9–18

Johns C (1995) The value of reflective practice for nursing. *J Clinical Nurs* 4: 23–30

Johns C (1996) The benefits of a reflective model of nursing. *Nurs Times* **92**(27):39–41

Kaberry S (1992) *Supervision - support for nurses? Sen Nurs* **12**(5): 38

Kargar I (1993) Whither supervision? *Nurs Times* **89**(40)22

Kramer M (1974) *Reality Shock.* Mosby, St. Louis.

Kohner N (1994) *Clinical Supervision in Practice.* King's Fund Centre, London.

Kohner N (1995) *Clinical Supervision an Executive summary* King's Fund Centre, London

Laing RD (1965) cited in Spleen SA (1993) *Safe Supervision, Interactions*, Autumn 93: 8

Laing W (1996) *Laing's Review of Private Healthcare.* Laing and Buisson Publication, London

Maggs C (1994) Mentorship in nursing and midwifery education: issues for research. *Nurs Educa Today.* **14**: 22–9

Mansfield B, Mitchel L (1996) *Towards a Competant Workforce.* Gower Publication, London

Marriott A (1991) The support, supervision and instruction of nurse learners in clinical areas: a literature review. *Nurs Educ Today* **11:** 261–9

Marken M, Payne M (1988) *Enabling and Ensuring: Supervision in Practice.* National Youth Bureau

Morton-Cooper A, Palmer A (1993) *Mentorship and Preceptorship A Guide to Support Roles in Clinical Practice.* Blackwell Scientific Publications, London.

Munroe H (1988) Modes of operation in clinical supervision. How clinical supervisors perceive themselves. *Br J Occupational Therapy* Oct **5**(10): 338–43

Nazarko L (1994) Nursing home nurses need support to update skills *Nurs Times* **92**(42): 38–40

NHS Executive (1996) *Clinical Supervision - A Resource Pack*

Nicklin P (1995) Super supervision. *Nurs Man* **2**(5): 24–5

Ooijen EV (1994) Whipping up a storm. *Nurs Stand* **9**(8):48

O'Toole A, Welt S (1994) *Interpersonal Theory in Nursing Practice: selected works of Hildegard Peplau.* Springer, New York

Paunonen M (1991) Promoting nursing quality through supervision. *J Nurs Staff Dev* **7**(5):229–33

Peutz B (1985) Learn the ropes from a mentor. *Nurs Success Today* **2**(6): 11–13

Platt-Koch L (1986) Clinical supervision for psychiatric nurses. *J Psych Nurs Men Health Services* **24**(1): 6–15

Proctor B (1988) *Supervision a working Alliance. (Video Tape Training Manual)* Alexia Publications, Leonards-on-sea, East Sussex

Proctor B (undated) Supervision: a cooperative exercise in accountability. In Marken M, Payne M (eds) *Enabling and Ensuring.* Leicester National Youth Bureau and Council for Education and Training in Youth and Community Work. Leicester pp 21-34

R.C.N. (1996) *Nursing Homes: Nursing Values.* Royal College of Nursing

Revicki D, May H (1989). Organisational characteristics, occupational stress and mental health in nurses. *Behav Med* **15:** 30–6

Rhodes L (1994) What can HCAs be asked to do? *Nurs Times* **90**(48): 33–4.

Rowden R (1992) More input required. *Nurs Times* **88**(33): 27–8

Rogers C (1957) The necessary and sufficient conditions of therapeutic personality change. *J Counselling Psych (USA)* **21**: 95–103

Rowan S (1987) *Supervison - The Reality Game.* Tavistock, London

Simms J (1993) Supervision. In W right H, Giddey M (eds) *Mental Health Nursing.* Chapman and Hall, London.

Snowball J, Ross K, Murphy K (1994) Illuminating dissertation supervision through reflection. *J Adv Nurs* **19:** 1234–46

Tingle T (1995) Clinical Supervision is an effective risk management tool. *Br J Nurs* **4**(14):794–5

Thomas S (1995) Clinical supervision. *J Com Nurs* Oct 12–18

United Kingdom Central Council for Nursing, Midwifery and Health Visiting (1992) *Code of Professional Conduct.* UKCC, London

United Kingdom Central Council for Nursing, Midwifery and Health Visiting (1993) The Council's Position Concerning a Period of Support and Preceptorship. *Registrar's Letter 1/1993, Annex one* UKCC, London.

United Kingdom Central Council for Nursing, Midwifery and Health Visiting (1993a) *Midwives Rules.* UKCC, London

United Kingdom Central Council for Nursing, Midwifery and Health VVisiting (1994) *The Midwife's Code of Practice.* UKCC, London

United Kingdom Council for Nursing, Midwifery and Health Visiting (1995) *Standards for Post-Registration Education and Practice (PREP)* UKCC, London

United Kingdom Central Council for Nursing, Midwifery and Health Visiting (1996) *Position Statement on Clinical Supervision for Nursing and Health Visiting.* UKCC , London

White E (1996) Clinical supervision and Project 2000: The identification of some substantive issues. *NT Research* **1**(2): 102–111

Wright B (1993) Clinical upervision. *A and E Nurs* 1(4): 181–2

Index

A

access 29
accountability 24, 30
accountable 30, 32
action plans 53
advanced practitioner 69, 80
advertisements 55
agenda 88–91
agreement 47, 50
Allitt enquiry 14
American10,12
Analyst113,129
APEL10
appraisal 26, 34, 109
pprehensive 99
pprenticeship 29
art 27
assess 32
assessment 48, 88
audit 18, 55, 110
audit tools 95
audited 59
authoritative 37, 85, 86
autonomous 128
autonomy 45, 123

B

baseline 59
benefit142, 43, 145, 146, 150, 152
boundaries 53,57,77
burnout 144
business world 151

C

care 20
capacity 33
catalytic 38, 86
cathartic 38, 86
chemistry75
child protection128
children's ward122
choice 42,74,118
choose 74
Choosing 55
client 36, 152
client supervision 23
clinical area146
clinical decisions 20
clinical nurse specialist105,120
clinical practice19,23,66,126
clinical risk management 150
clinical techniques 19
Clothier Report 122
coaching 10
collaboration40
colleagues 50
collusion103
comforting 27
commitment 33,98
communication33
community122
competence model 20
complaints110,146
compulsory 29–30
confidence 10, 19,34,106,145,148
onfident 148
confidential 25, 88– 89, 91

Confidentiality 37, 49, 53, 78, 82, 93, 95, 101, 121
confronting 38, 86
consumer protection15,150
contract 18,49,50,53,57,94,155
contracts 55,68
control 17, 54, 73,152
corporate organisations 138
cost 43,110,147
Counselling 27, 36, 38, 65, 69, 81, 91, 113, 129
counsellor 37, 74
crisis intervention 54
culture of nursing 23

D
decision 84, 88
decision-making 22
Department of Health 4, 14–16, 122
developed 98
developing 149
development 119
developmental models 58, 125
directing 23
disagreements 53
discuss 89
district nurse 110

E
employees 34, 135
employers 29, 34
enthusiasm 117
environment 84
ethical 93
ethics 36
evaluate 30, 35, 82, 146, 152
evaluation14,16,138,158
evaluator113,129
evidence based 55

expectations 47
experimental 152
expert 69

F
facilitated 98
faciliative 37, 85, 86
facilitator113,124,129
fears 106
feedback 25, 70, 73, 90, 107, 109, 117
first session 52
flattering 145
flexible 40
focus groups 59
formalised 25
formative 21, 22, 48, 58, 66, 84, 112, 129
Frankham's 12role model of supervisor functions 112, 129
function of supervision 58
functions 129

G
general practice 133
general practitioner133,137
groundrules 13, 47, 49, 50, 53, 73, 91, 93, 101-102, 126
group 115
group supervision 60, 63, 124, 131, 136
guidance 27,107
guidelines 52

H
health care assistants 41,43,117
health visitor 13,127, 131
helicopter view 39
helping relationships 29
hierarchical 13,23,34,123,133

hierarchical relationships 100
hierarchy 24,124
holistic 24
honest 99
hospital 50
hospital model of clinical super- vision 67

I

implementation47, 50, 96
independent homes 138
independent practitioners 133
individual performance review, 19, 34,54
informative 38,86
inspection 17
intensive care unit 124
interpersonal relationships 27
interpersonal skills 33, 69
investments 45
'it's my time' 117

J

job 145
job description 17

K

King's Fund Centre 66
knowledgeable 33

L

leadership 25, 45
learning disability group 116
learning process 6
life-time of learning 29
line manager 62,74,75,76
listening 69
local circumstances 13
local needs 13
local policies 17

low staffing 33
low visibility skills 27

M

maintaining 149
management 22,25, 54
management of change 108
manager 49,75–77,108,113,129
managerial 54,62,64,81, 93,133
managerial control 19,143
managerial supervision 13,42
managers 13, 44, 45, 50, 54, 67–68, 109,143, 151
managing 20–21
Manchester University 16
medical ward 107
meeting 83,88
mental health 105
mentee 10,151
mentor75
mentor7, 9,10,26,113,129,151
midwifery 35,79
midwifery practice 13
midwifery supervisor 35
midwives 13, 23
mirror 113,129
model of clinical supervision 26,46,58,61
monitor 113,129
monitoring 23– 24,119
monitoring process 6
motivation 50,100,108
motivator 124
mutual commitment 75

N

national vocational qualifications 41
negative feedback 22
network 63,120,134,136
network supervision114,130

nhs executive conference 19
non-managerial hierarchical 64
normative 21, 22, 58, 66, 84, 112, 129
nurse led units 138
nurse specialists 121
nursing development units 4
nursing home 119,138
nursing practice 24
nursing theory 24
nvq qualifications 118

O
objectives 34
off duty 116
off-duty rota108
openness 72
organisation 34
organisational goals 20
organisational objectives 150
outcome 25, 57,81
ownership 32,33

P
panacea153
paper exercise152
pastoral support 48
patient care 69,106
patient centre 24
patient focused 69
patient outcome 110,152
patient satisfaction 146
patient satisfaction surveys 153
patients interests 34
peer group 25,120,132,140
peer group supervision 60
peer groups 114,130
peer support 25,42
performance supervision 35

personal development 34, 64, 70, 103
personal problems 74
policy 50
policy change 40
portfolios 10
position statement on clinical supervision12
practice development nurses 105
practice nurses 133,135
practice nurse supervision 137
practitioners 66
preceptorship 7,10,11,26,29, 31
PREP 139
preparation74,81,134
prescriptive 38
prescriptive model 86, 87
primary nurses 123
principles 46,49
problem solving 60
problem solving tools 81
procedures 19
process models 61,64
professional development 13,24, 48,55,81,143
professional judgement 153
professional learning 10
professional portfolio 95
professional relationship 13,77
professional representation 113,129
professional support 4,38,125
protocols 53
psychotherapy 113,129

Q
qualified 41,47,57,124,148
quality 18

quality assurance 22,48,53
quality indicators 55
quantitative data147

R
randomised controlled trial 152
reality shock 11
ratio of supervisors 79
record keeping 49
records 18,53,92,94,95
re-evaluation 54
reflecting 13,19,39,40,41, 42,56,60,66,73,88,140
reflective diary 94
reflective practice 84
reflects 116
relationship 8–9,11,32,52
research 152
resource 79
resources 45
resources 44
responsibilities 41
restorative21,22,58,66,84, 112,129
restored 98
reviewer 113,129
reward 49, 72
role confli cts 78
role model70
role modelling 10

S
safety of care 15
satisfaction145
self 40
self assessment 4
self awareness 69,72
senior nurses 23
session 88,92,91,94
set ground rules 74
sickness rates 146

sister/charge nurse 122
six category intervention 37
skills development 64
social workers 122, 132
specialist expertise 111
specialists 115,127
speciality 123
staff nurse 105,116,124
staff performance 34
staff turnover18,151
staffing establishments 44
standard of practice125,126
standards 12,13,18,19,22–23, 41,53,64,70,79,83,149–150, 153
standards setting 64
statutory requirement 29
stresses 111,120,144
stressful 149
structural model 61
structure 54,57,61,107
students 9–10,30–31,33
students progress 32
supervise 143
supervised practice 24
supervisee 48,49,52,57,72,76, 77,81,92,94,96,100,102,126, 142,146,149
supervision 115
supervisor 47,49,52,57,69,71, 75,76,78,80,94,96,98,99,100, 102,108,115116,118123,126, 134,135,145
supervisors of midwives 23
support12,22,24,45,64–65,70, 107,119,149
supported 151
supporter 10
supportive11,42,133
supportive 38,86
supportive process 6
suspicion 93
system 124

T

tasks 19,84,88
talking therapies 27
target group 47
teacher 113,129
teaching 10,11
team 111,114,127
team meetings 26
team supervision 130
teamwork146
technical expertise 27
therapeutic expectation 36
therapeutic relationship 23, 36
therapist 36,113,129
threatening 42,63,135
time 49,54,59,67,74,79, 91,96,101,107,109,115,116, 121,126,142
time for me 8,9
time involvement 47
time out 29
top down 34
trained 41, 117
trainer113,129
training42,50,55,71,80–81, 98–99,108,109,119,135
training facilities18
transition period 11
triadic 63
Trust 10,43,66,149

U

UKCC 1984 92
UKCC PREP 1990 11
UKCC 1992 17,79
UKCC 1993 11
UKCC 1993a 13,23
UKCC 1994 13
UKCC 1995 139
UKCC 1996 3,4,12,19,23, 29,34,35,39,46,66,67,75,78, 92,136,150
unconditional positive regard 69
unit manager126
unqualified 41,47
untrained 41,117

V

vision 10
visionary 26
Vision for the Future 30,149

W

ward manager 24,107
ward sister 24
weaknesses 63,77
work environment 11